# BEYOND REASONABLE DOUBT

JAMES WHITAKER

LIFE PUBLISHING HOUSE

Copyright



Published by **Life Publishing House**

Printed in the United States of America

First Edition

*"Always be prepared to give an answer to everyone who asks you to give the reason for the hope that you have."*

1 Peter 3:15

# Prologue

Dr. Nathaniel Price knew the room was too full before he reached the podium. Students lined the walls of Harrington Hall with notebooks, laptops, coffee cups, and the restless energy of young minds waiting either to be challenged or offended. The lecture had been announced two weeks earlier as part of Northbridge University's annual public forum on truth and society, and the title alone had attracted far more attention than anyone in the philosophy department expected.

Some students had come because they admired Dr. Price. Others had come because they disagreed with him and wanted to challenge whatever argument he intended to make. A few had already positioned their phones to record before he even spoke, sensing that something controversial might happen. Several professors stood along the back wall with folded arms, curious enough to attend but cautious enough to remain spectators.

Dr. Price set his notes on the podium and looked over the crowded room. Thirty-two years of teaching had made him comfortable in front of students, but he had never grown careless. He knew ideas mattered. He had spent his career lecturing on Plato, Aristotle, Augustine, Aquinas, Hume, Kant, Nietzsche, Marx, and Darwin. His task had never been to tell students what they had to believe. He had always considered his responsibility to be something simpler and far more demanding. He wanted them to think honestly and to follow truth wherever it led, even when it challenged their assumptions.

He waited until the room settled.

"I want to begin by saying something clearly," he said. "I am not here to ask anyone to turn off their mind. Questions are not dangerous. Doubt is not a sin. If truth is real, then it should never be afraid of honest examination."

The sound of typing spread through the room. Several students opened laptops. Others reached for pens.

"For many people," he continued, "faith means believing without evidence or even believing against evidence. I understand why people think that way. Religion has often been presented in those terms, and when it has, it deserves criticism. But that is not what I mean by faith. I am speaking about trust grounded in reason, evidence, and history."

A hand rose near the front.

"Dr. Price, are you saying belief in God can be proven?"

He recognized the student immediately.

"Not in the same way we prove a mathematical equation," he answered. "Most conclusions in life are not reached that way. Historians, scientists, doctors, and jurors weigh evidence and ask which explanation best accounts for the facts. My argument is that belief in God belongs in that category. It can be rationally defended."

The answer produced mixed reactions. Some students nodded. Others exchanged skeptical glances. A few smiled as though they had already prepared counterarguments.

Dr. Price turned a page in his notes.

"The universe had a beginning. Space, time, matter, and energy are not eternal in the way many once believed. If the universe began to exist, then we naturally ask why there is something rather than nothing. We ask what caused the beginning itself. Questions like these have occupied philosophers and scientists for centuries."

He moved carefully through the material. He spoke about the remarkable order of the cosmos and the information contained within DNA. He distinguished complexity from information and explained why many thinkers considered the existence of life itself worthy of deeper reflection. He was not trying to force agreement. He was presenting arguments and inviting scrutiny.

When he moved to morality, the atmosphere in the room changed.

"Every one of us lives as though certain things are truly right and certain things are truly wrong. We may disagree over moral issues, but disagreement itself assumes that something objective exists. When we condemn cruelty, oppression, or abuse, we are doing more than expressing personal preference. We are appealing to standards that we believe transcend individual opinion."

Another hand rose.

"Are you saying atheists can't be moral?"

"No," Dr. Price replied immediately. "Many atheists live moral lives, and some do so with admirable consistency. The question is not whether people recognize moral truth. The question is what makes moral truth real if human opinion is all that exists."

The room grew quieter. Students who had been checking phones earlier now paid closer attention.

He paused before continuing.

"The most difficult question, however, is suffering. If God exists, why do children die? Why does evil prosper? Why do good people suffer? I have no interest in pretending these questions are easy. They are not. But I would suggest that when we call something evil, we are acknowledging that good exists and that reality ought to be different than it is."

He saw several faces change. The room had become less argumentative and more reflective.

"Christianity does not begin by pretending suffering does not exist," he said. "It begins with the claim that God entered suffering. It presents a Savior who experienced grief, injustice, betrayal, and death. Whether one accepts that claim or rejects it, it deserves to be examined seriously."

Near the back of the room, Dr. Eleanor Richards entered quietly. She had intended to stop by for only a few moments before leaving for another meeting, but the sight that greeted her caused her to pause. Every seat was occupied. Students sat on the floor. Others stood along the walls. Nobody appeared eager to leave.

She remained near the door and listened.

Dr. Price eventually moved to the center of his argument.

"Ultimately, Christianity rests upon a historical claim. It rises or falls on the person of Jesus Christ. If Jesus remained in the grave, Christianity collapses. If He rose from the dead, then history itself forces us to reckon with His identity."

Someone near the back laughed softly.

"So that's what this really comes down to?"

Dr. Price smiled.

"It always has."

The room erupted into questions, and what was scheduled to be a ninety-minute lecture stretched into more than two hours. Students challenged him on science, philosophy, morality, and the problem of evil. Some questions were sharp, others deeply personal. A young woman whose mother had died from cancer asked whether prayer mattered when heaven seemed silent. A philosophy major objected to objective morality. A biology student challenged intelligent design.

Dr. Price answered patiently. Sometimes he pointed to philosophers and historians. Sometimes he admitted uncertainty. He never mocked objections, and he never acted threatened by disagreement. More than once he acknowledged that some questions remained difficult, but he insisted that difficulty did not excuse people from examining the evidence.

By the time the lecture ended, clusters of students had gathered around the podium. Some thanked him. Others continued arguing. No one seemed indifferent.

Near the doorway, Professor James Carlisle approached Dr. Richards with visible concern.

"I think he crossed a line," he said quietly.

Dr. Richards kept her eyes on the crowd surrounding Dr. Price.

"What line do you think he crossed?"

"He teaches philosophy, Eleanor. Religious conclusions don't belong in the classroom."

She remained silent for a moment.

"I saw arguments," she finally said. "I saw evidence. I saw students asking questions. I'm not sure that's what concerns people."

Carlisle frowned.

"Then what does concern them?"

Dr. Richards watched as another student stepped forward to continue questioning Dr. Price.

"I think some people are afraid students might actually listen."

Neither of them realized that half a dozen phones had recorded the lecture. Neither imagined that clips would spread across the country before nightfall. And neither could have known that one afternoon in Harrington Hall would eventually place twelve strangers in a jury room where they would be forced to decide far more than the future of a philosophy professor.

# BEYOND REASONABLE DOUBT

# 1

David Stone stood in front of the mirror and adjusted his tie for the third time. At sixty years old, he had learned that trials were rarely won once the lawyers stood before the jury. They were won in preparation, discipline, and the quiet hours when no one was watching. He had argued before appellate courts, represented clients whose reputations had been nearly destroyed, and spent thirty-five years navigating the legal profession with steady hands. As he studied his own reflection that morning, a deep uneasiness settled over him, the kind that did not come from fear of losing, but from knowing that the case waiting for him would reach far beyond the parties named in the lawsuit.

The phone on the dresser vibrated, and David reached for it without taking his eyes off the mirror. It was Nathan Cole, his junior associate, already stationed near the courthouse and trying to sound calm. "David, they're already gathering outside," Nathan said, his voice tight with pressure. David looked toward the window and tightened the knot of his tie. "They're early," he said, though something in Nathan's voice told him the morning had already moved past ordinary expectations.

“No, sir,” Nathan said. “They’ve been there since four this morning.”

David glanced at the clock on the nightstand and saw that it was only six thirty. “How many?” he asked, already knowing the answer would not be small.

“Thousands, maybe more by the time court opens,” Nathan said. “Police have the courthouse blocked off on three sides, and every network has a crew outside.”

David closed his eyes for a moment, gathered himself, and returned his focus to the room. “I’ll be there in thirty minutes. Keep the team together, and do not talk to anyone from the press.”

He ended the call and remained where he was, his hand still resting on the phone. His eyes drifted to the framed photograph beside the lamp, and for a moment the pressure of the trial gave way to the familiar ache of memory. Sarah had been gone four years, though twenty-eight years of marriage had made her voice part of the furniture of his mind. She used to tell him that truth did not need defending as much as people needed reminding. After cancer took her, David had spent night after sleepless night wrestling with questions he had once dismissed, questions about suffering, purpose, eternity, and God.

Those questions had not led him to easy answers. They had led him to books, debates, ancient texts, scientific arguments, and a long season of private humility. He had not come to faith because grief needed a crutch or because religion offered him comfort. He had come to faith because he believed the evidence pointed somewhere real, and because reality had a way of remaining firm even when a man resisted it. The sound of helicopters passed over the building, and David walked to the window as news aircraft circled above the downtown skyline.

"What in the world have we become?" he said quietly.

Across town, Rebecca Kane sat in the back seat of a black SUV as it moved through morning traffic toward the courthouse. Her eyes were fixed on the city passing behind the tinted glass while her assistant reviewed notes beside her. He had a tablet open, a trial binder on his lap, and three different news feeds running at once. Rebecca did not need any of it. She had memorized every argument, every motion, every evidentiary ruling, and every witness sequence before most of the country had finished reading the headlines.

The driver glanced into the rearview mirror. "Traffic is backed up for miles around the courthouse."

Rebecca did not answer at first because she was watching a line of protesters pass along the sidewalk with signs raised above their heads. Her assistant, Mark Ellis, tried to sound casual as he closed one file and opened another. "They're calling this the Trial of the Century," he said.

Rebecca looked at him with a faint expression of irritation. "They called three others that before lunch yesterday."

Mark gave a nervous smile and adjusted his glasses. "Are you nervous?"

Rebecca turned back toward the window. "No. Irritated."

"Because people think they already know how this should end?"

Rebecca shook her head slightly. "Because everyone thinks this case is about religion. It isn't."

Mark let the statement settle before asking the obvious question. "Then what is it about?"

Rebecca continued staring out the window as the courthouse district came into view. "It is about whether a university has the right to punish a professor for conclusions it does not like."

Mark closed the file in his lap and looked at her more carefully. "That almost sounds like you agree with Stone."

"I agree that the issue has to stay narrow," she said. "This is a civil lawsuit, not a national referendum on God."

As they approached downtown, the crowds became impossible to ignore. Protesters lined both sides of the street, some holding signs that declared God was the answer and others insisting religion was the problem. Television crews occupied entire intersections, and satellite trucks stretched along the curb in a row of steel, cables, and floodlights. Commentators spoke into cameras with the confidence of people who had already reduced the case to slogans. By the time Rebecca's vehicle reached the secured entrance, the country had already formed arguments of its own.

Inside the courthouse, Judge Eleanor Hayes sat in chambers reading the final briefs one more time. Forty years on the bench had taught her that every case carried consequences, even when the lawyers pretended otherwise. Some cases affected families, others affected communities, and a few reached beyond the parties named in the caption. This case, she suspected, belonged in that last category. The pleadings were precise, the claims were civil, and the public meaning attached to the lawsuit had become larger than anything the court could control.

Her clerk entered with a tablet in one hand and a stack of updated security notes in the other. "Judge, every major network is outside, and the overflow room is already full," he said.

Judge Hayes kept reading for another moment before removing her glasses. "Expected."

"They're estimating tens of millions following the coverage today."

Hayes placed the brief on her desk. "Tens of millions of opinions, and not one of them sitting in the jury box."

The clerk gave a polite smile, though his concern remained visible. "The nation is watching."

Judge Hayes stood and reached for her robe. "The nation always watches. The question is whether anyone is listening."

The clerk hesitated near the door. "Do you think people are ready for what they're about to hear?"

Hayes looked toward the courthouse corridor. "People have been putting God on trial for centuries. Today they will hear a civil case about whether a professor was punished for speaking what he believed the evidence allowed him to say."

By eight o'clock, the courthouse had become nearly inaccessible. Local law enforcement had placed barricades around the plaza, and deputies checked credentials at every controlled entrance. No cameras were allowed inside the courtroom, although the court had authorized a closed audio feed to an overflow room and a public transcript release at the end of each day. Outside, reporters spoke as though the case had already become a national referendum. Online commentators declared winners and losers before the bailiff had called the room to order.

David stepped from his car at the secured entrance and paused long enough to take in the crowd. Questions came from every direction, overlapping until they became noise rather than speech. "Mr. Stone, do you believe you can prove God exists?" one reporter shouted. Another called out, "Is faith compatible with science?" David gave no answer, only a brief nod as the deputies opened the barrier and guided him through. He had learned long ago that courthouse steps were dangerous places for lawyers who liked the sound of their own voices.

Inside, the building carried a different kind of tension. The marble floors, high ceilings, and controlled voices made the courthouse feel removed from the chaos outside, though everyone inside knew the pressure had followed them through the doors. David passed through security, greeted his team, and reviewed the order of proceedings one final time. The judge would address preliminary matters, remind both sides of the evidentiary boundaries, and then bring in the jury. After that, the whole country would hear opening statements filtered through transcripts, commentary, and whatever each side chose to say once court adjourned.

David stopped when he saw Rebecca approaching from the opposite end of the hall. She was dressed in a dark suit, carrying no visible notes, and walking with the calm precision that had made her one of the most respected defense lawyers in higher-education litigation. For a moment, neither spoke, though the noise around them continued. Rebecca reached him first and gave a professional nod. "David."

"Rebecca."

She looked toward the courtroom doors, then back at him. "You ready?"

"Ready enough."

"That does not sound like confidence."

David adjusted the file under his arm. "Confidence is not the same thing as certainty. I have seen too many trials to confuse the two."

Rebecca gave a slight smile. "Then we may agree on something after all."

David studied her for a moment, aware that her calm had edges she rarely showed in public. "We agree more than you think. We both believe truth matters."

Rebecca's smile faded just enough to be noticed. "People speak, David. Evidence speaks only when lawyers know how to use it."

David nodded, accepting the point without surrendering his own. "Evidence can be misused. So can language. That does not make truth negotiable."

Rebecca shifted her trial binder to her other hand. "Truth is what survives examination."

David looked toward the courtroom doors as the bailiff appeared inside the vestibule. "Truth is what remains whether we examine it honestly or not."

The bailiff opened the courtroom doors and addressed the attorneys waiting in the hall. "Counsel, the court is ready."

David and Rebecca stepped forward with their teams, each carrying years of training, private wounds, and carefully prepared arguments into a room built for order. The gallery was full, the jury room was occupied, and Judge Hayes was already on the bench reviewing the first matter on the docket. At counsel table, Professor Daniel Price sat quietly beside David, his hands resting near a closed notebook and a worn leather Bible he had agreed not to display before the jury. Across the aisle, representatives of the university sat behind Rebecca, composed in the practiced manner of institutions that believed procedure could protect them from the human cost of their decisions.

Outside, the crowd kept chanting, cameras kept rolling, and the country kept arguing with itself. Inside, the case would proceed the only way a civil trial could proceed, one claim, one objection, one witness, and one piece of evidence at a time. The caption on the pleadings did not say God versus the University. It said Price versus Westbridge University. Judge Hayes intended to make sure the jury remembered that.

# 2

By nine o'clock, the plaza surrounding the United States District Courthouse looked less like the opening day of a civil trial and more like a national event. Satellite trucks lined the streets for several blocks, their cables taped across sidewalks and guarded by production assistants wearing network badges. Protesters stood behind metal barricades, some holding signs that read "Faith Is Freedom," while others lifted banners demanding "Reason Over Religion." Local police and federal marshals kept the entrances clear, directing credentialed press through one checkpoint and court personnel through another. News anchors stood on temporary platforms across the street, speaking with the certainty of people who had only minutes to explain issues that had taken centuries to form.

Inside Studio A at the National Broadcast Center in New York, veteran journalist Michael Reynolds adjusted his earpiece and glanced at the red light above the main camera. In thirty years of reporting, he had covered wars, elections, natural disasters, congressional hearings, Supreme Court nominations, and civil trials that became national symbols. He had seen public attention gather around major cases before, though this one carried a pressure he found difficult to name. Every major network had cleared part of its morning schedule, and several streaming platforms were carrying live analysis from outside the courthouse. Schools, churches, universities, and civic groups had already announced forums to discuss the proceedings after court recessed.

A producer stood behind the camera and counted down the final seconds before the broadcast. Lisa Grant, Michael's co-anchor, leaned toward him and spoke quietly enough that only he could hear. "Hard to believe the whole country is stopping to watch a civil lawsuit," she said. Michael glanced at the notes in front of him and then at the monitor showing the courthouse plaza. "It says something about the case," he replied. Lisa followed his eyes toward the screen and asked, "What does it say?" Michael adjusted the papers on his desk and answered, "It says people know there is more at stake than one professor and one university."

The red light came on, and Michael turned toward the camera with the practiced calm of a man who understood the size of the moment. "Good morning. I'm Michael Reynolds, and we begin today with the civil trial that has drawn national attention unlike anything this federal courthouse has seen in decades. The legal issues are narrow, and the court has made clear that this case will be decided by evidence, testimony, and the law, not by public opinion. Professor Daniel Price claims Westbridge University punished him for conclusions he reached and expressed in connection with his academic work. The university denies wrongdoing and maintains that its actions were based on professional standards, institutional policy, and the boundaries of scholarship."

By the time the broadcast began, people were watching from places that had little else in common. In Dallas, a retired Baptist pastor turned up the volume while his wife carried coffee into the living room. In Boston, a philosophy professor gathered his graduate students around a conference table and told them to listen less like spectators and more like scholars. In Los Angeles, producers paused their morning meetings and watched the live feed from the courthouse steps. In airport lounges, diners, offices, prison dayrooms, military bases, and college libraries, conversations slowed as the coverage continued.

Inside the courthouse, Rebecca Kane sat at the defense table reviewing her notes with the same discipline that had carried her through every major trial of her career. The gallery behind her was full, though no television cameras had been allowed inside the courtroom. Reporters sat shoulder to shoulder with legal pads open, while a sketch artist worked near the back row under the careful eye of court security. Rebecca could hear the muffled sound of the crowd outside whenever the heavy doors opened. Her attention remained on the binder in front of her until her eyes paused on a photograph tucked inside one of the inner pockets.

Her father stood behind a church pulpit in the photograph, smiling with one arm around her shoulders. Rebecca had been sixteen when it was taken, wearing a dress she remembered hating and a smile she remembered forcing. Six months later, the affair became public, and the life her family had built inside that church began to collapse in full view of everyone they knew. The denials came first, then the admissions, then the meetings, then the split that divided friends, families, and entire rows of pews. The whispers followed Rebecca long after the church had found another pastor and moved on without apology.

Rebecca closed the binder and slid the photograph out of sight. She reminded herself that truth was not found in old pain, family history, or feelings that returned without permission. Facts mattered, evidence mattered, and competent lawyers did not confuse personal wounds with legal arguments. She had built her career on that principle, and it had served her well in courtrooms where sentiment often tried to disguise itself as proof. Still, as she rested her hand on the closed binder, she knew some memories did not need permission to rise.

Across the hall, David Stone sat alone in a small attorney conference room reserved for the plaintiff's team. His Bible rested beside a stack of legal documents, though he had not opened it since arriving at the courthouse. He did not need to search for the verse that had occupied his thoughts all morning. Pilate's question from the Gospel of John had stayed with him from the moment he woke. What is truth?

David leaned back in his chair and let the question settle in the quiet room. Two thousand years earlier, another trial had taken place before a judge who thought he held authority over the matter before him. A crowd had gathered, accusations had been made, and political pressure had pressed itself into the shape of justice. Pilate had stood face to face with truth and treated Him as though He were merely another defendant. David sat with that thought for a moment, then lowered his eyes to the trial notebook in front of him.

Nathan Cole knocked once and entered, carrying a tablet and a yellow legal pad. "Sir, every network is covering this live from outside the courthouse," he said. David nodded without looking up from the page. Nathan came farther into the room and added, "Some analysts are saying the audience could pass one hundred million before the end of the day." David closed the notebook and said, "People are paying attention." Nathan looked at the tablet and asked, "To the lawsuit?" David answered, "To what the lawsuit represents."

Nathan shifted his weight, still looking like a young lawyer who had not yet learned how much silence belonged in a courthouse. "I think most of them are watching because it is controversial," he said. David placed the notebook into his trial bag and checked the tabs on the first witness outline. "Controversy can draw a crowd," he said. "Questions about truth can keep people listening." Nathan nodded, though David could tell the younger man was trying to decide whether the answer was strategy, faith, or both. Before either of them spoke again, the courtroom deputy stepped into the hallway and called for counsel to report to Courtroom One.

David gathered his files, and Nathan opened the door for him. The hallway was controlled by federal marshals, with reporters held behind a marked line near the public entrance. Questions rose as the attorneys approached, though none of the lawyers answered. David kept his eyes forward as camera crews outside the interior security doors filmed through the glass from a distance. The marshal checked credentials one final time, opened the courtroom door, and directed the plaintiff's team inside.

The courtroom carried a weight that had nothing to do with volume. The public gallery was full, the press section had reached capacity, and the jury waited in the box under instructions not to speak about the case or consume outside coverage. The judge had prohibited phones, cameras, and recording devices, leaving reporters with notebooks, memory, and the official transcript that would be released according to court order. Rebecca sat at the defense table with her team arranged beside her, while David took his place at the plaintiff's table and set his files in order. The room was not loud, though every person inside seemed aware that the world outside was trying to enter.

Professor Daniel Price sat beside David in a dark suit, his posture controlled and his face pale under the courtroom lights. He had spent most of his adult life in lecture halls, laboratories, faculty meetings, and academic conferences, not in a federal courtroom with millions of people waiting to interpret his every word. The university's representatives sat behind Rebecca, composed and careful, dressed with the neutral confidence of an institution accustomed to committee rooms and polished statements. A civil caption identified the parties in plain language: Daniel Price v. Westbridge University. Outside the courthouse, almost no one seemed interested in keeping the case that narrow.

The courtroom deputy rose and addressed the room. "All rise. The United States District Court for this district is now in session, the Honorable Eleanor Hayes presiding."

Judge Hayes entered from chambers, took her seat behind the bench, and looked over the courtroom before instructing everyone to be seated. She reviewed the docket sheet, glanced at both counsel tables, and then turned her attention to the jury. Her expression was calm, controlled, and firm enough to remind everyone present that public interest did not alter courtroom procedure. She placed both hands near the edge of the bench and spoke with the measured authority of someone who expected to be obeyed.

"This court is aware of the extraordinary attention surrounding these proceedings," Judge Hayes said. "Let me remind everyone present that we are not gathered here for entertainment, ratings, politics, or personal agendas. This is a court of law, and this civil case will be tried according to the rules of evidence and the instructions of this court. The plaintiff will have the opportunity to present his claims, the defendant will have the opportunity to present its defense, and the jury will consider only what is properly admitted in this courtroom. Public opinion has no place in your deliberations, and commentary outside these walls is not evidence."

Judge Hayes paused long enough to let the instruction reach the jury box. "The eyes of the nation may be upon this case, though that cannot be your concern," she continued. "Majorities can be wrong, institutions can be wrong, lawyers can be wrong, and judges can be wrong. Your responsibility is not to measure popularity. Your responsibility is to listen carefully, weigh the evidence honestly, follow the law as I give it to you, and reach a verdict rooted in reason and integrity." Neither David nor Rebecca moved as the judge finished speaking.

Outside the courtroom, millions followed reports from anchors, analysts, commentators, professors, pastors, skeptics, and activists who each believed they understood the larger meaning of the case. Inside the courtroom, twelve ordinary citizens had been asked to do something far less dramatic and far more difficult. They had been asked to listen. David looked down at his notes, Rebecca opened her binder, and Judge Hayes turned to the first page of the trial schedule. Price v. Westbridge University would now proceed.

# 3

Judge Eleanor Hayes waited until the jurors were seated and the courtroom had settled before she leaned slightly toward the microphone. The deputy had finished checking the gallery, counsel had returned to their tables, and the official court reporter sat ready with her hands near the stenograph machine. Judge Hayes looked first at the jury box, then briefly toward counsel. She wanted the room to understand that the attention outside the courthouse would not change the rules inside it. This was a civil lawsuit, and the jury's duty would be to decide the claims between Professor Daniel Price and Westbridge University based only on the evidence admitted in court.

"Ladies and gentlemen," she began, "opening statements are not evidence. They are not testimony, they are not exhibits, and they are not proof. They are each side's opportunity to tell you what they believe the evidence will show during the course of this civil trial. Your duty is to listen carefully, weigh the testimony, examine the admitted evidence, and follow the law as I give it to you. You must not decide this case based on public opinion, personal feelings, media coverage, or the arguments of counsel."

The jurors watched her closely, some with pens ready, others sitting with steady attention as the judge spoke. Judge Hayes continued in the same measured voice. "The lawyers are advocates, and you should expect them to present their positions with skill and conviction. What they say is not evidence unless it is supported by testimony or exhibits admitted in this courtroom. If your memory of the evidence differs from what either lawyer says, your memory controls. With that instruction in mind, Ms. Kane, you may proceed with the defense opening statement."

Rebecca Kane rose from the defense table and buttoned her jacket as she stepped into the open space before the jury. She carried a thin folder to the lectern, placed it down, and rested one hand lightly on the edge of the podium. Her voice was calm, controlled, and free of theatrical force. She had tried enough cases to know that jurors often trusted restraint more than volume. When she began, she spoke to them as twelve citizens asked to decide a serious civil dispute, not as spectators at a national event.

"Ladies and gentlemen of the jury, this case is not about whether people have the right to believe in God," Rebecca said. "They do. It is not about whether religion has brought comfort to grieving families, strength to suffering people, or moral direction to communities. It has. It is not about whether churches and people of faith have done good in the world. Many have, and Westbridge University is not asking you to decide otherwise."

She stepped away from the lectern and moved a few feet closer to the jury box. "The question before you is narrower and more precise. Professor Daniel Price did not merely say that he personally believes in God. He publicly claimed, in connection with his academic position, that belief in God is supported by objective facts and evidence. He told students that morality requires God, that science points toward God, and that Christianity is not simply meaningful or personally helpful, but true. Those statements were not presented as private convictions. They were presented as academic conclusions."

Rebecca let the words settle before continuing. "You will hear from scientists, historians, philosophers, theologians, and experts in several fields. Some will speak with impressive credentials, and some will use language that sounds persuasive. They will tell you the universe points to a Creator, that morality needs a Lawgiver, and that Jesus Christ rose from the dead. They will ask you to treat Christianity not merely as faith, but as established fact. Ladies and gentlemen, belief is not evidence, conviction is not proof, and sincerity does not turn a religious claim into objective academic knowledge."

She glanced briefly toward Professor Price, who sat beside David Stone with his eyes fixed on the jury. "This case began when Westbridge University determined that Professor Price crossed a professional boundary. The university concluded that presenting religious belief as objective truth in a public academic setting violated the standards expected of those entrusted with educating students. You will hear that the university did not act because Professor Price privately believed in God, attended church, read Scripture, or lived according to his faith. It acted because he used his academic role to present disputed religious claims as settled truth."

Rebecca returned to the lectern and turned a page she did not need to read. "Mr. Stone will tell you this case is about free speech, censorship, and courage. He will tell you Professor Price was punished for following evidence where it leads. The evidence will show something more specific. This case is about whether a public academic institution may maintain standards that distinguish between personal belief and objective instruction. It is about whether claims of faith can be placed in the same category as academic knowledge simply because the person making them believes deeply."

She looked from one juror to the next, allowing her argument to remain firm without sounding angry. "You will hear extraordinary claims in this courtroom. Extraordinary claims require careful evidence, not assumptions, not tradition, and not emotional appeal. You will hear theories, interpretations, historical arguments, and philosophical reasoning. At the end of this trial, we believe the evidence will show that faith belongs to the realm of personal conviction, not objective fact. We believe you will conclude that Professor Price presented belief as certainty when the evidence did not justify that claim."

Rebecca gathered her folder and gave the jury a respectful nod. "Your verdict will not decide whether people may believe in God. That right is secure. Your verdict will decide whether Westbridge University acted within its responsibility when it required academic claims to meet academic standards. When all the evidence is in, we are confident you will find that the university acted lawfully and reasonably." She returned to the defense table, placed her folder beside her binder, and sat without looking toward David.

Judge Hayes made a brief notation on the pad before her and turned toward the plaintiff's table. "Mr. Stone, you may proceed."

David Stone rose slowly, not for effect, but because years of trial work had taught him never to hurry the first moment a jury truly studied him. He carried only a yellow legal pad, though most of the page remained blank. He approached the lectern, set the pad down, and looked at the jurors for a moment before speaking. His voice was steady, and his tone carried the discipline of a lawyer who knew the case would be won by clarity, not volume. Professor Price sat behind him, quiet and still, with the restrained posture of a man whose life's work had been placed before strangers for judgment.

"Ladies and gentlemen, Ms. Kane is correct about one important thing," David began. "This case is not about the right to believe whatever we want. Truth is not determined by preference, popularity, or personal comfort. If something is true, it remains true whether a person believes it or not. If something is false, sincerity cannot make it true."

He moved one step away from the lectern, keeping his posture relaxed and his voice even. "You have just heard that faith and facts belong in separate worlds. You have heard that religious claims may provide comfort, meaning, and private guidance, while objective truth belongs somewhere else. That is one of the central assumptions this case will ask you to examine. Professor Price did not ask his students to stop thinking. He asked them to consider whether reason, science, morality, history, and human experience point beyond themselves."

David turned slightly toward Professor Price, then back to the jury. "This case began because Professor Daniel Price made a statement that has become unpopular in some circles. He said truth exists. He said morality is not created by majority vote. He said belief in God is not blind faith, but a conclusion supported by evidence. For making those claims in an academic setting, he was investigated, disciplined, and removed from the work he had spent his life doing."

He returned to the lectern and placed one hand on the edge of it. "Over the next several weeks, you will hear testimony from experts in cosmology, biology, philosophy, ethics, archaeology, history, and textual criticism. You will hear from people who disagree sharply with one another. Some will believe in God, others will not. Some will be Christians, others will be skeptics. The plaintiff is not asking you to suspend reason. We are asking you to use it."

David glanced briefly toward Rebecca, then continued without raising his voice. "Ms. Kane and her team will challenge our witnesses. They should. Cross-examination is not an enemy of truth. Honest questions are not a threat to truth. In this courtroom, claims should be tested, evidence should be examined, and conclusions should be reached carefully. That is not something Professor Price fears. That is exactly what he asked Westbridge University to allow."

He lifted his legal pad, glanced at it once, and set it down again. "You will hear evidence that the universe had a beginning. You will hear testimony about fine-tuning, the origin of life, consciousness, human dignity, and the moral law written into human experience. You will hear arguments about whether good and evil are real, or only names we give to preferences. You will examine historical evidence surrounding the New Testament documents, the life of Jesus of Nazareth, His crucifixion, and the claim that He rose from the dead. These are serious matters, and they deserve more than slogans from either side."

David paused long enough to let the jurors follow him without feeling pushed. "If Christianity is false, then it should not be protected from examination. If Jesus Christ did not rise from the dead, then Christians have believed something that is not true. The apostle Paul himself said as much nearly two thousand years ago. Professor Price did not claim Christianity should be accepted without evidence. He claimed the evidence deserved to be heard, weighed, and discussed in the same academic environment where every other worldview is examined."

He looked toward the bench for a moment, then back to the jury. "Every courtroom in this country operates on the assumption that truth exists and can be discovered. We call witnesses because truth matters. We admit exhibits because truth matters. We allow cross-examination because truth matters. We ask juries to render verdicts because facts can be weighed, evidence can be tested, and reasonable conclusions can be reached. The entire justice system depends upon that foundation."

David's tone softened slightly, though his words remained precise. "At the end of this trial, we will not ask you to believe that every mystery has been solved or that every difficult question has disappeared. We will ask you to decide whether the evidence supports the conclusions Professor Price reached. We will ask whether belief in God must be confined to private opinion, or whether reason permits a person to conclude that

God exists. We will ask whether a university may punish a professor because his conclusions point toward God."

He picked up the legal pad and held it at his side. "Truth has never needed protection from honest investigation. It has survived empires, tribunals, revolutions, universities, skeptics, believers, and generations of people who were certain their age had finally settled the matter. This case is not an invitation to turn off your mind. It is an invitation to use it fully. When the evidence is complete, we trust you will find that Westbridge University crossed the line from academic oversight into unlawful punishment." David nodded to the jury, then returned to the plaintiff's table and sat beside Professor Price.

Judge Hayes looked down at her notes and gave both sides a moment before speaking. "Very well. The court will take a fifteen-minute recess. Members of the jury, please remember my earlier instructions. Do not discuss the case with anyone, do not allow anyone to discuss it with you, and do not read, watch, or listen to any media coverage concerning these proceedings. When we return, we will begin with the plaintiff's first witness."

The deputy called the room to order as Judge Hayes left the bench, and the courtroom slowly shifted from formal silence into controlled movement. Jurors were escorted out through a side door, while attorneys gathered exhibits, whispered to assistants, and reviewed the next stage of the morning. Rebecca remained seated at the defense table, marking a passage in her witness outline and preparing for the first round of testimony. Across the aisle, David leaned toward Professor Price and spoke quietly before both men turned their attention back to the proceedings. The openings had defined the battlefield, and when court resumed, the case would move from promises to proof.

# 4

THE COURTROOM SETTLED AS the jurors returned from the morning recess and took their seats. Judge Eleanor Hayes waited until the deputy closed the side door and the court reporter placed her fingers above the keys. David Stone stood at the plaintiff's table with his notebook open, while Professor Daniel Price sat beside him and watched the bench. Rebecca Kane had a faculty handbook open in front of her at the defense table, marked with tabs and yellow highlights. The gallery was quiet, though the tension in the room had not eased.

Judge Hayes looked over the courtroom before turning to David. "Mr. Stone, you may call the plaintiff's first witness," she said. Her voice was calm, and it brought every conversation in the gallery to an immediate stop. David closed his notebook and rose from his chair. He gave Professor Price a small nod before turning toward the bench. "The plaintiff calls Professor Daniel Price, Your Honor."

Price stood and walked to the witness stand with the steady pace of a man who had spent most of his adult life in front of classrooms. The witness chair was different from a lecture hall, and everyone in the room seemed to understand that difference. The deputy administered the oath, and Price answered clearly before taking his seat. David waited until the microphone was adjusted before he approached the lectern. He rested his legal pad in front of him and looked at the witness with a measured calm.

"Professor Price, let's begin with your work at Northbridge University," David said. "How long did you teach there?"

"Thirty-two years," Price said. "Most of that time was spent teaching philosophy, ethics, and the history of ideas."

"When you say philosophy and ethics, what kind of questions were your classes dealing with?"

Price looked toward the jury before answering. "Questions about truth, morality, human nature, reason, suffering, meaning, and the ideas that shape civilizations. Those are not small subjects, and I never treated them as small."

A few jurors began writing, and David gave them time. "Before the lecture involved in this lawsuit, had Northbridge University ever disciplined you?"

"No."

"Had anyone ever accused you of grading students based on whether they agreed with your personal conclusions?"

"No," Price said. "Students were graded on how well they understood the material, how carefully they reasoned, and whether they could defend a position."

David stepped away from the lectern, keeping his voice conversational. "What happened when a student disagreed with you?"

Price gave the faintest smile, as though the question reminded him of better days. "I usually told them to make the argument stronger. Agreement was never the standard in my classroom. Serious thought was. Some of my best students disagreed with me, and I respected them for it."

David let the answer settle before moving on. "Did you ever require students to attend church, pray, participate in religious services, or take part in any faith-based activity connected to your courses?"

"No," Price said. "I taught in a university classroom."

"Then tell the jury what happened with the lecture at issue in this case."

Price's expression grew more careful. He shifted slightly in the witness chair and looked toward the jury. "The lecture was titled Truth, Morality, and Meaning in a Scientific Age. I argued that belief in God was intellectually defensible. I argued that science, morality, consciousness, history, and human dignity raise questions that materialism does not fully answer. I told the students the arguments should be examined, challenged, and tested."

David glanced down at his notes. "Were you asking students to accept those conclusions without thinking?"

"No," Price said. "That would defeat the purpose of teaching philosophy."

"Then what were you asking them to do?"

"Think carefully," Price answered. "Ask hard questions. Follow the argument and decide whether it holds together. A conclusion is not dangerous because it points toward God. It is only dangerous if no one is allowed to examine it."

Rebecca Kane stood before David had fully returned to his chair. She carried a thin folder and the marked faculty handbook to the lectern. Her movements were measured, and her voice remained even. "Professor Price, this lecture took place during a regularly scheduled Northbridge University class, correct?"

"Yes."

"It was not a chapel service."

"No."

"It was not a church event."

"No."

"It was not a private religious seminar."

"No," Price said. "It was a philosophy class."

Rebecca opened the faculty handbook and turned it so the witness could see the exhibit. "You recognize Joint Exhibit 12 as the Northbridge faculty handbook?"

"I do."

"You were familiar with the policy requiring professors to distinguish established academic consensus from contested interpretation and personal religious conclusion."

"Yes."

"You understood that policy before giving the lecture."

"I understood the policy."

Rebecca let the handbook remain open. "During that lecture, you told students that morality ultimately requires God."

Price leaned toward the microphone. "I argued that objective moral obligation is difficult to ground without God."

Rebecca did not blink. "That was not my question. Did you tell your students that morality ultimately requires God?"

Price looked at her for a moment. "Yes, in the context of the argument I was making."

Rebecca nodded slightly and moved to the next point. "You also told them Christianity is true."

"I argued that Christianity withstands rational examination."

"Professor Price, did you affirm Christianity as true?"

"Yes."

"And did you affirm the resurrection of Jesus Christ?"

"Yes," Price said. "As a historical claim."

The answer seemed to tighten the room. Rebecca turned another page in the transcript and read silently for a moment. "The class recording shows that you spent a substantial portion of the lecture defending Christian conclusions."

"I spent that portion examining philosophical and historical arguments."

"Arguments that led to Christianity."

"Arguments that led where I believed the evidence led."

Rebecca stepped away from the lectern so the jury could see Price clearly. "You were not hired by Northbridge to teach theology, were you?"

"No. I was hired to teach philosophy, ethics, and the history of ideas."

"And students registered for your course expecting philosophy."

"Yes."

"Several students complained after the lecture."

"Yes."

Rebecca let that answer sit before continuing. "The university investigated those complaints, and administrators met with you afterward."

"Yes."

"They asked you to clarify that your religious conclusions reflected your personal convictions rather than objective academic fact."

"That was the wording they wanted," Price said.

"And you refused."

"I refused to use wording I believed was inaccurate."

Rebecca's voice lowered slightly, and the question sounded less like accusation and more like pressure. "Northbridge was not asking you to deny your faith, Professor Price. It was asking you to distinguish faith from fact in a public academic classroom."

Price remained composed. "I do distinguish faith from fact. I do not accept the premise that faith has no relationship to evidence."

"You understood the university believed you had crossed a professional boundary."

"I understood the university objected to my conclusion and to the way I stated it."

Rebecca gave him no time to expand. "You also understood refusal could lead to discipline."

"Yes."

"And after that warning, you still declined to issue the clarification requested by the university."

"Yes."

Rebecca closed the folder and returned to the defense table. "No further questions at this time, Your Honor."

David rose for redirect and returned to the lectern. He did not rush, and that seemed to steady the room. "Professor Price, Ms. Kane asked you about academic boundaries. During your years at Northbridge, were you ever instructed to stop discussing Aristotle?"

"No."

"Kant?"

"No."

"Nietzsche, Marx, Freud, or Darwin?"

"No," Price said. "Those thinkers were part of the curriculum."

David placed the handbook on the lectern. "Does this policy prohibit professors from reaching conclusions?"

"No," Price said. "Philosophy requires conclusions to be stated, tested, criticized, and defended."

"Were your students free to reject your conclusions?"

"Always."

"Were they penalized for doing so?"

"Never," Price said. "A student could disagree with me completely and still earn a strong grade if the reasoning was careful."

David kept his hand on the lectern. "Did you present opposing viewpoints in class?"

"Yes, and not as decorations."

Some jurors looked up at the phrase. Price continued before David asked the next question. "They were central to the course. Students cannot examine a claim honestly if they never hear the strongest objections to it."

David nodded. "If a professor argues that morality evolved through natural selection, is that a philosophical conclusion?"

"Yes."

"If a professor teaches that truth is relative, is that also a conclusion?"

"Yes."

David began to ask another question, and Rebecca rose. "Objection, Your Honor. Argumentative."

Judge Hayes looked toward David. "Sustained. Rephrase the question."

David accepted the ruling with a brief nod. "Yes, Your Honor." He turned back to Price. "In your discipline, may professors present competing views and explain why one view appears stronger than another?"

"Yes," Price said. "That is ordinary philosophical instruction."

"Did you tell students they had to become Christians to succeed in your class?"

"No."

"What did you tell them would affect their grade?"

"Weak reasoning, unsupported claims, careless reading, and failure to engage opposing arguments," Price said. "Their personal agreement with me was never part of the grading standard."

David paused, then asked the question slowly. "Why did you refuse the university's directive?"

Price looked toward the jury. "Because the directive required me to describe my conclusions as personal preference. That would have been dishonest. I reached those conclusions through years of reading, debate, study, criticism, and examination. I would correct a factual error. I would not reclassify a reasoned conclusion because administrators were uncomfortable with it."

David's voice softened. "Are you asking this jury to accept Christianity without evidence?"

"No," Price said. "If Christianity is false, no one should believe it."

"Why?"

"If Jesus Christ did not rise from the dead, Christianity collapses as a truth claim," Price said. "I believe it is true because I believe the evidence supports it."

"Do you welcome scrutiny of that conclusion?"

"Yes," Price replied. "Truth does not need shelter from honest examination."

David returned to counsel table and placed his legal pad beside his notebook. "No further questions, Your Honor."

Judge Hayes looked toward Rebecca. "Anything further?"

Rebecca rose enough to answer clearly. "Nothing further, Your Honor."

The judge turned to the witness. "Professor Price, you may step down."

Price thanked the court, left the witness stand, and returned to his seat beside David. Rebecca made a notation in her witness outline and spoke quietly to her associate. The jurors watched Price cross the room, and several wrote something before the next witness was called. Judge Hayes looked toward Rebecca once the courtroom settled again. "Ms. Kane, you may call the defendant's next witness."

Rebecca stood and faced the bench. "The defense calls Dr. Charles Bennett."

A distinguished man in his early sixties rose from the second row behind the defense table and walked to the witness stand. For more than thirty-five years, Bennett had taught philosophy and ethics at Stanford University, and his scholarship had been cited by religious and secular writers alike. He described himself as an agnostic, and his reputation rested on seriousness, patience, and intellectual fairness. After the oath was administered, he adjusted the microphone and waited for Rebecca to begin. Rebecca approached the lectern with a different folder and gave him a respectful nod.

"Dr. Bennett, you heard Professor Price testify that objective truth and morality ultimately point to God," Rebecca said. "Do you agree with him?"

Bennett answered with the calm precision of a professor used to careful distinctions. "I agree that objective truth exists. I do not agree that belief in God is necessary to recognize it."

"Would you explain that to the jury?"

Bennett turned slightly toward them. "Science depends on truth. Logic depends on truth. Historical claims are accurate or inaccurate. This courtroom assumes truth exists every time a witness takes an oath."

Rebecca moved to the subject of morality. "Does morality require belief in God?"

"No," Bennett said. "Morality can be understood through human flourishing, empathy, reason, social obligation, and our shared humanity."

"Can a person live a moral life without believing in God?"

"Certainly. Many people do."

"In your opinion, did Professor Price violate accepted academic standards in the lecture?"

"Yes," Bennett said. "Professors should distinguish evidence, interpretation, and personal philosophical or religious conclusion, especially when teaching students in a university classroom."

David rose for cross-examination with only a few notes. "Good afternoon, Dr. Bennett."

Bennett gave him a polite nod. "Good afternoon."

"You agree objective truth exists."

"I do."

"You also agree morality is real, not merely taste or preference."

Bennett paused briefly. "Yes, I believe morality is real."

David rested one hand on the lectern. "So the disagreement is what ultimately grounds truth and morality."

"That is a fair way to state it."

"Why is murder wrong?"

"Because it destroys human life, violates human well-being, and attacks the conditions necessary for community."

"Why does human well-being matter?"

"Because human beings possess dignity."

David did not interrupt. "What gives human beings dignity?"

Bennett looked down briefly before answering. "Our shared humanity, our capacity for reason, our relationships, our vulnerability, and our nature as conscious moral agents."

David listened without expression. "Were the Nazis morally wrong?"

Rebecca stood at once. "Objection, Your Honor. Relevance and inflammatory."

David turned toward the bench. "Your Honor, the witness has testified about universal morality. I am testing the foundation of that opinion."

Judge Hayes considered the objection. "Overruled as to relevance. Keep the question focused, Mr. Stone."

David nodded. "Yes, Your Honor."

Bennett answered after a brief pause. "Yes. The Nazis were morally wrong."

"Wrong because modern society disapproves of them, or wrong in a deeper sense?"

"Wrong in a deeper sense."

"According to what standard?"

"Universal moral principles," Bennett said. "Human dignity, and the wrongness of cruelty, domination, and murder."

David looked down at his notes, then back at the witness. "Where do those universal principles come from?"

Bennett answered honestly. "That remains one of philosophy's most difficult questions."

David gave no visible reaction. "Dr. Bennett, professors defend conclusions every day, correct?"

"Yes."

"When a professor argues that materialism best explains reality, that is a conclusion."

"Yes."

"When a professor argues that religious belief lacks sufficient evidence, is that also a conclusion?"

"Yes," Bennett said. "Depending on how it is framed."

"Should that professor be allowed to defend the conclusion if opposing views are fairly presented?"

"Yes."

David moved from theory back to Price's classroom. "Based on the materials you reviewed, did Professor Price prevent students from disagreeing with him?"

"No."

"Did he punish dissenting students?"

"I saw no evidence of that."

"Did he conceal opposing views?"

"The course materials I reviewed included opposing views."

David paused before his next question. "So your disagreement is not that Professor Price refused debate. Your disagreement is that you believe he overstated his conclusion."

Rebecca rose again. "Objection. Counsel is testifying."

Judge Hayes looked toward David. "Sustained. Ask questions, Mr. Stone."

David nodded and adjusted his approach. "Dr. Bennett, should questions concerning God be excluded from academic examination because they are religiously significant?"

"No," Bennett said. "They should be examined carefully."

"Should students be allowed to hear arguments for and against those claims?"

"Yes, with appropriate academic framing."

David gave a slight nod. "Thank you, Doctor. No further questions."

Rebecca stood for redirect and kept her binder closed. "Dr. Bennett, when you say questions concerning God may be examined, do you mean professors may present religious conclusions as settled academic fact?"

"No," Bennett said. "I mean those questions may be examined through argument, evidence, and competing positions, with the professor making clear where the scholarly consensus ends and where personal conclusion begins."

"In your opinion, did Professor Price exercise that level of caution?"

"Not sufficiently."

Rebecca nodded. "Nothing further."

Judge Hayes looked toward David. "Any recross?"

David stood again. "Briefly, Your Honor." He turned to Bennett. "Dr. Bennett, if a professor makes clear that a conclusion is contested and then explains why he believes the evidence supports it, is that automatically outside academic standards?"

"No," Bennett said. "Not automatically."

"So the issue is not whether the subject may be discussed. The issue is fairness, framing, and whether students are allowed to challenge the conclusion."

"Yes."

David returned to his seat. "No further questions."

Judge Hayes turned to the witness. "Dr. Bennett, you may step down."

Bennett thanked the court and left the witness stand with the same composed manner he had brought to it. At counsel table, Professor Price leaned closer to David and kept his voice low. "I am not sure that helped us."

David watched Bennett return to his seat. "It helped more than you think."

"How?"

"He conceded objective truth, moral reality, the legitimacy of examining God in a university classroom, and the right of professors to defend contested conclusions with proper framing."

Judge Hayes glanced at the clock and addressed the courtroom. "We will recess for lunch. Members of the jury, remember my instructions. Do not discuss the case with anyone, do not read about it, and do not allow anyone to speak with you about it. Court will reconvene at one-thirty."

The deputy directed everyone to rise as the judge left the bench. The jurors filed through the side door while the attorneys gathered exhibits and reviewed their notes for the afternoon session. The morning testimony had placed truth, morality, and academic freedom before the jury in practical terms. David remained at counsel table, reviewing the next witness outline while Price sat beside him in silence. Across the aisle, Rebecca was already preparing for the afternoon, where each side would try to give those ideas legal weight.

# 5

THE COURTROOM RECONVENED SHORTLY after lunch, and the controlled quiet returned slowly as reporters hurried back to their seats and spectators settled into the gallery. Judge Eleanor Hayes reviewed her notes from the morning session while the court reporter adjusted her machine and the deputy checked the side door leading to the jury room. Questions concerning truth and morality had occupied much of the first day, but the testimony was now moving into a different arena. Philosophers could debate ideas at length, though science demanded evidence, definitions, and careful limits. If Professor Price was correct, then the plaintiff would need to show that belief in God was not merely private conviction, but a conclusion he believed reason and evidence permitted him to defend in an academic setting.

Judge Hayes looked toward the plaintiff's table. "Mr. Stone, you may call your next witness."

David stood and buttoned his jacket. "Your Honor, the plaintiff calls Dr. Benjamin Carter."

A distinguished man in his late sixties approached the witness stand with a measured, careful walk. He had spent more than forty years studying astrophysics and cosmology and had taught at several major universities. His research had earned broad respect, though his later public arguments had made him controversial among colleagues who believed he had moved too close to theology. He had argued in books, lectures, and interviews that modern cosmology did not eliminate the question of God. In his view, it made the question harder to avoid.

The deputy administered the oath, and Dr. Carter answered clearly before taking his seat. David waited while the microphone was adjusted, then approached the lectern with a slim folder and a yellow legal pad. He did not open either one right away. The jurors watched the witness closely, perhaps sensing that the afternoon testimony would ask them to consider science in a case that had already become larger than employment, policy, and academic procedure. David rested one hand on the lectern and began.

"Dr. Carter, would you tell the jury your field of expertise?" David asked.

"I am a professor emeritus of astrophysics," Carter said. "My research has focused on cosmology, which is the study of the origin, structure, and development of the universe."

"How long have you worked in that field?"

"Over forty years."

David nodded and gave the jurors a moment to write. "Dr. Carter, is it accepted within modern science that the universe had a beginning?"

"Yes," Carter said. "That is the mainstream scientific understanding."

"Has that always been the case?"

"No. For much of the twentieth century, many scientists preferred an eternal-universe model. An eternal universe avoided the question of a beginning in the same way. As the evidence developed, those models became much harder to defend."

David stepped slightly away from the lectern. "What evidence are you referring to?"

"The expansion of the universe," Carter said. "Edwin Hubble's observations showed that distant galaxies are moving away from us and from one another. If you reverse that expansion mathematically, you move toward an earlier state when the universe was far denser and hotter. That points to a beginning of the universe as we know it, including space, time, matter, and energy."

"What is that beginning commonly called?"

"The Big Bang."

David looked briefly toward the jury. "Does the Big Bang prove God?"

"No," Carter said.

"It does not?"

"No. Science does not prove God in the way mathematics proves a theorem. It can point toward certain conclusions and make some explanations more reasonable than others. The Big Bang does not place God under a microscope. It does raise the question of why the universe exists at all."

David let the answer settle. "What do you mean by that?"

"If the universe began to exist, then it is reasonable to ask what caused it to exist," Carter said. "Things do not bring themselves into existence. Whatever caused space, time, matter, and energy cannot simply be another object inside space, time, matter, and energy. The cause would have to be beyond the universe in some meaningful sense."

David kept his voice even. "What qualities would such a cause have?"

"It would be timeless, since time itself is part of the universe," Carter said. "It would be immaterial, since matter is part of what began. It would have to possess power adequate to bring the universe into existence. It would also be independent of the universe, rather than dependent on the universe for its own existence."

David turned a page on his legal pad, though he did not appear to read from it. "Are those qualities consistent with what classical theism means by God?"

"Yes," Carter said. "They are consistent with that conclusion."

David returned to the lectern. "No further questions."

Judge Hayes looked toward the defense table. "Ms. Kane, you may cross-examine."

Rebecca rose with a thin folder in one hand and moved to the lectern. She did not rush, and she did not appear irritated. Her calm gave the exchange a sharper edge than anger would have. She placed the folder down, opened it to the first marked page, and looked directly at the witness.

"Dr. Carter, are you telling this jury that God caused the Big Bang?" Rebecca asked.

"I am saying the evidence points toward a transcendent cause."

"Science cannot observe that cause directly, can it?"

"No, not directly."

"So your conclusion is philosophical."

"It is philosophical, and it is also informed by science."

Rebecca picked up a page from her folder. "Would you agree that science has often explained things that people previously attributed to God?"

"Certainly," Carter said. "That has happened many times."

"Lightning, disease, eclipses, storms, and earthquakes were all explained religiously by various cultures before science provided natural explanations."

"Yes, in many cases."

"So why stop now?"

"I am not stopping inquiry," Carter said. "I am saying the beginning of the universe raises a question that natural processes inside the universe may not fully answer."

Rebecca stepped slightly away from the lectern. "Yet you conclude God."

"I conclude that the evidence points beyond nature."

"Would you agree that other scientists look at the same evidence and do not reach your conclusion?"

"Yes."

"Would you agree that your conclusion is disputed?"

"Yes," Carter said. "Many important conclusions are disputed."

Rebecca closed the folder. "No further questions."

Judge Hayes looked toward David. "Any redirect?"

David stood just enough to answer. "No, Your Honor."

Judge Hayes thanked Dr. Carter and excused him from the witness stand. Carter stepped down and walked past the jury box without looking toward either counsel table. Rebecca remained standing as the witness left the courtroom. She waited until the room settled again before addressing the bench.

Judge Hayes glanced at the trial schedule and then looked toward her.

"Ms. Kane, does the defense intend to call a witness in response?"

"Yes, Your Honor. The defense calls Dr. Alan Pierce."

A tall man with silver hair rose from the second row behind the defense table and approached the witness stand. Dr. Alan Pierce was one of the world's leading cosmologists and a frequent critic of theistic arguments drawn from science. His books on physics and the universe had become international bestsellers, and his lectures had made him a familiar public voice in debates over cosmology. He carried himself with the ease of a man accustomed to hostile audiences and complicated questions. After taking the oath, he sat comfortably and adjusted the microphone.

Rebecca approached the lectern with a different folder. "Dr. Pierce, do you agree that the universe had a beginning?"

"I do," Pierce said.

"Do you agree with Dr. Carter's conclusion that this beginning points toward God?"

"No, I do not."

"Why?"

"Because a beginning does not necessarily imply God," Pierce said. "It means the universe, as we understand it, had an early state that requires explanation. There are natural models under consideration, and science continues to investigate those possibilities. An unanswered question should not be treated as a completed theological conclusion."

Rebecca nodded. "Could you explain some of those models?"

"There are models involving quantum cosmology, eternal inflation, and multiverse theories," Pierce said. "Some propose that our observable universe may be part of a larger physical reality. Others explore whether the beginning of our universe is a boundary of our current model rather than an absolute beginning of everything that exists. These are difficult questions, and no responsible scientist should pretend they are simple."

"So invoking God is unnecessary?"

"At best, premature."

"Would saying 'God did it' risk ending scientific inquiry?"

"It can," Pierce said. "Science advances by continuing to ask questions, testing models, and refusing to stop at explanations that cannot be examined further."

Rebecca paused, then looked toward the jury. "In your opinion, did Professor Price have sufficient scientific basis to present belief in God as an objective conclusion from cosmology?"

"No," Pierce said. "He had a philosophical interpretation of scientific evidence. That is different from an established scientific conclusion."

Rebecca returned to the lectern. "No further questions."

Judge Hayes turned toward the plaintiff's table. "Mr. Stone, you may cross-examine."

David stood and approached the lectern slowly. He greeted the witness with a polite nod, and Pierce returned it. David understood the value of this witness. Dr. Pierce was not careless, angry, or easily dismissed. He was serious, qualified, and careful enough to concede what the evidence did and did not show.

"Good afternoon, Dr. Pierce," David said.

"Good afternoon."

"You and Dr. Carter agree that the universe had a beginning."

"Yes."

"And you agree that space, time, matter, and energy came into existence in connection with that beginning."

"That is the standard view, yes."

David glanced at his notes. "You mentioned multiverse theories. How many universes have we directly observed?"

Pierce smiled slightly. "One."

"So no direct observations of other universes?"

"No direct observations."

"No experiments confirming them?"

"No."

"No measurements taken from them?"

"No."

"Then the multiverse remains theoretical."

"Yes," Pierce said. "It remains theoretical, though there are models that some believe support it indirectly."

David nodded, accepting the precision. "A theoretical possibility can still be worth exploring."

"Certainly."

"You also mentioned quantum explanations. Quantum fluctuations occur in quantum fields, correct?"

"Yes."

"And quantum fields are something."

"They are physical realities described by theory, yes."

"So when people say the universe came from nothing, they usually do not mean nothing in the ordinary sense."

Pierce smiled again. "Usually not. The word nothing is often used carelessly in public discussions."

David walked a few feet before the jury box, careful not to make the movement feel staged. "Dr. Pierce, if someone told this jury that an unseen and unobservable collection of universes exists beyond our own and helps explain why our universe appears finely arranged for life, would that require an inference?"

"Yes," Pierce said. "It would be an inference from a theoretical framework."

"Evidence or inference?"

"Both, depending on how the argument is made. At this stage, much of it remains inference."

"So both you and Dr. Carter are making inferences from the evidence."

"That is fair."

"The difference is that Dr. Carter infers an intelligent cause, while you infer a broader natural reality that has not been directly observed."

Pierce considered the wording. "That is simplified, but not unfair."

David returned to the lectern. "Dr. Pierce, do you believe science explains everything?"

"No."

"It does not?"

"No. Science is powerful, but it has limits."

"Can science fully explain why there is something rather than nothing?"

"No."

"Can science fully explain consciousness?"

"Not at present."

"Can science establish objective morality through measurement alone?"

"No," Pierce said. "Science can study moral behavior, but it cannot by itself establish moral obligation."

David let that answer sit for the jury. "So science itself has limits."

"It does."

David looked at his notes one last time, then closed the folder. "No further questions."

Judge Hayes looked toward Rebecca. "Any redirect?"

Rebecca stood. "Briefly, Your Honor."

She returned to the lectern and faced Dr. Pierce. "Dr. Pierce, when you say science has limits, does that mean every philosophical or religious conclusion becomes a scientific conclusion?"

"No," Pierce said. "A limit in science does not automatically validate a particular religious claim."

"Does your testimony mean questions about God cannot be discussed in a university?"

"No. They can be discussed, especially in philosophy, history, religion, and related disciplines. The issue is how they are framed."

Rebecca glanced toward the jury. "And in your opinion, how should they be framed?"

"As contested interpretations," Pierce said. "Not as settled scientific conclusions."

Rebecca nodded. "Nothing further."

Judge Hayes looked toward David. "Anything further, Mr. Stone?"

David rose. "One question, Your Honor."

Judge Hayes nodded. "Proceed."

David looked back at Pierce. "Dr. Pierce, if a professor clearly presents a conclusion as contested, explains the evidence supporting it, and allows students to challenge it, would the subject be outside academic inquiry simply because the conclusion points toward God?"

Pierce paused before answering. "No. Not simply because it points toward God."

David gave a small nod. "Thank you, Doctor. No further questions."

Judge Hayes thanked Dr. Pierce and excused him from the stand. He stepped down with the same calm he had carried into the courtroom, passed the defense table, and left through the side door. Judge Hayes looked at the clock, then toward the jury. The afternoon had moved carefully, though the questions beneath the testimony had not become easier.

"We will take a fifteen-minute recess," Judge Hayes said. "Members of the jury, remember my instructions. Do not discuss the case with anyone, and do not read, watch, or listen to any coverage concerning these proceedings."

The deputy escorted the jurors out through the side door, and the courtroom released the low murmur it had been holding back. Dr. Price leaned toward David at the plaintiff's table while Rebecca organized her files across the aisle. David remained seated, making a note beside the next witness outline. Price kept his voice low enough that only David could hear him.

"You did not attack him," Price said.

"There was no reason to."

"He disagrees with almost everything I said."

"He also answered honestly."

Price looked toward the empty witness stand. "You let him make his case."

David closed his pen and slipped it into his jacket pocket. "Truth does not fear questions."

Across the room, Rebecca placed Dr. Pierce's outline back into her binder and spoke quietly with Mark Ellis. She respected Pierce, and she believed he had defended the university's position well. Still, she could not ignore what both scientists had admitted under oath. Neither side disputed that the universe had a beginning. The disagreement was not over that fact, but over what kind of explanation the fact permitted.

Judge Hayes remained on the bench for a moment after counsel began gathering papers. She had heard many expert witnesses during her career, and the honest ones always made trials more difficult. They refused to fit neatly into the categories lawyers preferred. Dr. Carter and Dr. Pierce had not given the jury certainty. They had given them the harder task of weighing evidence, inference, and the limits of explanation.

When the recess ended, the testimony would move from the origin of the universe to the question of why it appeared so precisely arranged for life. Judge Hayes glanced toward the jury room door, then down at her notes. The first witness had raised the question of origin. The next would raise the question of design.

# 6

WHEN COURT RECONVENED THE following morning, Judge Eleanor Hayes noticed that the atmosphere had changed. The testimony concerning the origin of the universe had generated discussion among the jurors, though none of it had taken place where anyone in the courtroom could hear it. Even the reporters in the press section seemed quieter, as if the previous day's testimony had made the public argument outside the courthouse feel less certain. The question before the jury was no longer whether the universe had a beginning. Both Dr. Benjamin Carter and Dr. Alan Pierce had agreed on that point, and their disagreement centered on what explanation the evidence permitted.

Judge Hayes reviewed the witness list and looked toward the plaintiff's table. The testimony would now move to a related question, one that crossed from cosmology into biology and the conditions necessary for life. If the universe had a beginning, the jury would now hear why that universe appeared to be so remarkably suited for living things. The issue was not whether the court would decide a scientific controversy for the world. The issue was whether Professor Price had acted outside academic standards by treating those scientific questions as evidence worthy of philosophical discussion.

"Mr. Stone," Judge Hayes said. "You may call the plaintiff's next witness."

David rose from the plaintiff's table. "Your Honor, the plaintiff calls Dr. Elizabeth Monroe."

A woman in her early fifties approached the witness stand with a professional calm that drew the jury's attention before she said a word. Dr. Elizabeth Monroe had spent nearly thirty years as a molecular biologist and genetic researcher. Her work in cellular biology and DNA sequencing had earned international recognition, and while she was publicly known as a Christian, her professional reputation rested on decades of laboratory research and peer-reviewed publications. She took the oath, answered clearly, and waited while the deputy adjusted the microphone. David approached the lectern with a thin folder and placed it beside his legal pad.

"Dr. Monroe, would you briefly describe your field of expertise?" David asked.

"I am a molecular biologist," Monroe said. "My research focuses on genetics, cellular systems, and the way biological information functions inside living organisms."

"How long have you worked in this field?"

"Nearly thirty years."

David glanced toward the jury before continuing. "Dr. Monroe, yesterday the jury heard testimony concerning the beginning of the universe. Today I want to ask a different question. Is life easy to produce?"

Monroe gave a faint smile, though her answer remained serious. "No. Life depends upon an extraordinary combination of factors."

"What do you mean by that?"

"The laws of physics, the strength of gravity, the electromagnetic force, the expansion rate of the universe, the masses of subatomic particles, the properties of carbon, the Earth's distance from the sun, and many other conditions exist within extremely narrow ranges," Monroe said. "If some of those values were changed even slightly, the universe would not permit life as we know it. In biology, we also see extraordinary coordination inside living systems. Life requires not only matter, but ordered information, functional structures, and conditions that allow those systems to operate."

David gave the jurors time to write before continuing. "What is the broader term often used for the narrow physical conditions that allow life?"

"The fine-tuning of the universe."

"Is the existence of fine-tuning itself disputed?"

"No," Monroe said. "The fine-tuning itself is widely acknowledged. The debate concerns what best explains it."

David moved one step from the lectern. "What explanations are commonly offered?"

"Some argue that the fine-tuning is the result of chance," Monroe said. "Others propose multiverse theories, suggesting that if there are enough universes, one like ours might eventually occur. Others see evidence of design. The disagreement is not usually over whether the conditions are striking. The disagreement is over what those conditions mean."

David turned a page in his notes. "In your scientific work, have you also studied biological information?"

"Yes."

"Would you explain DNA for the jury?"

"DNA functions in some ways like a language or code," Monroe said. "It contains instructions necessary for life. Those instructions are used by cellular machinery to build proteins and regulate biological processes. Every cell in the human body contains information far beyond what scientists imagined generations ago. The more we learn about life at the molecular level, the more remarkable the information systems become."

David remained near the lectern. "Why does biological information matter to this discussion?"

"Because information is not the same thing as mere complexity," Monroe said. "A pile of rocks can be complex in one sense, but it does not contain coded instructions. DNA contains sequences that perform functions. When we encounter coded information in every other area of experience, we naturally ask where that information came from."

David looked toward the jury. "In your experience, what does information usually point toward?"

Rebecca rose before Monroe could answer. "Objection, Your Honor. Calls for a broad conclusion and risks inviting the witness to offer a theological opinion as scientific fact."

David turned toward the bench. "Your Honor, I am asking the witness to explain the basis for her scientific and philosophical inference. The university's position is that Professor Price crossed an academic boundary by discussing these issues.

The jury is entitled to hear whether such inferences are made from evidence."

Judge Hayes considered the objection. "Overruled in part. The witness may answer as to her reasoning and professional experience. The jury will understand that the answer is offered as opinion testimony, not as a ruling by this court on the ultimate truth of the matter."

David nodded. "Thank you, Your Honor."

Monroe looked back toward the jury. "In my experience, information consistently points to intelligence. That does not mean every scientist agrees with my conclusion. It means that when I consider the fine-tuning of the universe and the information contained in living systems, design is the explanation I find most persuasive."

David allowed the answer to settle before continuing. "Are you saying scientific questions should stop because you believe design is the best explanation?"

"No," Monroe said. "Science should continue asking questions. Design is not an excuse to stop investigating. It is an inference about what the evidence most reasonably suggests."

David closed his folder. "No further questions."

Judge Hayes looked toward the defense table. "Ms. Kane, you may cross-examine."

Rebecca approached the lectern with a folder. Her expression remained neutral, though her questions came with the precision of a lawyer who knew exactly where she wanted to go. "Dr. Monroe, you are a Christian, correct?"

"I am."

"And your Christian faith affects the way you view the world."

"It affects my worldview," Monroe said. "Just as atheism, agnosticism, or materialism affects the worldview of others."

Rebecca nodded slightly. "So your conclusions are influenced by your beliefs."

"As everyone's conclusions are," Monroe replied. "That does not mean evidence is irrelevant."

Rebecca opened her folder. "Dr. Monroe, is it possible that life arose through natural processes?"

"Possible, yes."

"And many scientists believe it did."

"Many do."

"So the science is not settled."

"Science is rarely settled in the way public debates suggest," Monroe said. "There are questions with stronger evidence and weaker evidence, but the origin of life remains deeply contested."

Rebecca stepped closer to the jury box while keeping her attention on the witness. "Would you agree that disagreement among scientists matters in a university classroom?"

"Yes."

"Would you agree that students should understand when a conclusion is contested?"

"Yes."

"And would you agree that presenting a contested interpretation as established fact can mislead students?"

"It can," Monroe said. "Depending on how it is presented."

Rebecca looked down at the page before her. "So if Professor Price presented design as the only academically responsible conclusion, that would be a problem."

David rose. "Objection, Your Honor. Hypothetical not tied to the witness's review of the lecture."

Judge Hayes looked toward Rebecca. "Ms. Kane?"

"I will rephrase."

"Sustained as phrased."

Rebecca turned back to Monroe. "Based on the materials you reviewed, did Professor Price tell students that his conclusion was contested?"

"Yes," Monroe said. "He discussed objections and competing views."

"But he also told them he believed the evidence pointed toward God."

"Yes."

Rebecca closed the folder. "No further questions."

Judge Hayes looked toward David. "Any redirect?"

David rose. "Briefly, Your Honor."

He returned to the lectern and looked at Monroe. "Dr. Monroe, does the fact that a conclusion is contested mean it cannot be discussed in a university classroom?"

"No."

"Does the fact that a conclusion has religious implications automatically make it academically improper?"

"No."

"What matters?"

"The evidence, the framing, the fairness to opposing views, and whether students are free to question the conclusion," Monroe said.

David nodded. "No further questions."

Judge Hayes thanked Dr. Monroe and excused her from the stand. Monroe stepped down, passed the jury box, and returned to the gallery. Rebecca reviewed the next witness outline with Mark Ellis before addressing the bench. Judge Hayes looked toward her over the top of her notes. The room settled again as the defense prepared to respond.

"Ms. Kane, you may call the defense's next witness."

"The defense calls Dr. Karen Simmons."

A woman in her late forties approached the witness stand with a confident, composed stride. Dr. Karen Simmons was a professor of evolutionary biology at Oxford University and one of the leading voices in abiogenesis research. She had spent decades studying the origin of life and had become known for challenging intelligent design arguments in academic and public settings. After taking the oath, she waited for the deputy to adjust the microphone. Rebecca approached the lectern and gave her a brief, respectful nod.

"Dr. Simmons, do you agree that life is complex?" Rebecca asked.

"Absolutely."

"Do you agree that the universe appears finely tuned for life?"

"Yes," Simmons said. "That appearance is part of the discussion."

"But you reject intelligent design."

"I do."

"Why?"

"Because apparent design does not necessarily require a designer," Simmons said. "Complex systems can arise through natural processes. We do not yet understand everything concerning the origin of life, but science continues to uncover answers. A mystery is not the same as evidence for design."

Rebecca nodded. "Do gaps in our knowledge prove God?"

"No."

"Do they prove design?"

"No."

"In your opinion, should a university treat intelligent design as settled science?"

"No," Simmons said. "It may be discussed in philosophy, religion, history of ideas, or as a cultural movement. It should not be presented as established biology."

Rebecca looked toward the jury. "Why is that distinction important?"

"Because students need to know the difference between a scientific theory, a philosophical interpretation, and a religious conclusion," Simmons said. "Those categories may interact, but they are not identical. A professor can discuss arguments for design. The problem comes when those arguments are presented as though they carry the same status as established scientific findings."

Rebecca returned to the lectern. "No further questions."

Judge Hayes turned toward the plaintiff's table. "Mr. Stone, you may cross-examine."

David approached the lectern with only a few notes. "Good morning, Dr. Simmons."

"Good morning."

"You agree the universe appears finely tuned."

"Yes."

"And you agree that DNA contains extraordinary information."

"Yes."

"You reject intelligent design because you believe natural explanations may exist."

"Correct."

David looked down at his notes. "Have scientists successfully created life from nonliving matter under conditions that establish how life originally arose?"

"No."

"Have scientists fully explained the origin of genetic information?"

"Not completely."

"Have scientists demonstrated how the first cell arose?"

"No."

"Do we currently possess a complete explanation for abiogenesis?"

"No," Simmons said. "We do not have a complete explanation."

David let the answer sit without changing his tone. "So some of the most important questions remain unanswered."

"Yes."

David turned a page on his legal pad. "You testified that complexity can arise naturally. Would you agree that information is different from complexity?"

"Yes."

"A snowflake is complex."

"It is."

"But it contains no coded instructions."

"Correct."

"A strand of DNA contains instructions."

"Yes."

"And in every other area of human experience, information originates from intelligence."

Simmons paused. "In human experience, yes."

David nodded. "So when Dr. Monroe infers design from information, she is making an inference based upon known experience."

"That would be fair," Simmons said.

"Just as you infer natural explanations based upon your scientific expectations and research commitments."

Simmons gave a slight smile. "That would also be fair."

David looked briefly toward the jury before continuing. "Dr. Simmons, is it improper for a professor to tell students that the origin of life remains an open question?"

"No."

"Is it improper to discuss competing explanations?"

"No."

"Is it improper to explain why some scientists or philosophers find design persuasive, provided opposing views are also presented?"

"No," Simmons said. "That can be discussed if it is framed properly."

David paused, then asked the question carefully. "Based on the materials you reviewed, did Professor Price tell students that there were opposing views?"

"Yes."

"Did he tell them they were free to reject his conclusions?"

"Yes."

"Did you see evidence that he punished students for disagreeing with him?"

"No."

David closed his notes. "No further questions."

Judge Hayes looked toward Rebecca. "Any redirect?"

Rebecca rose. "Briefly, Your Honor."

She returned to the lectern. "Dr. Simmons, when you say these issues may be discussed with proper framing, does that mean Professor Price's framing was necessarily proper?"

"No," Simmons said. "A subject can be appropriate for discussion while still being handled improperly."

"In your opinion, did he handle it properly?"

"Not entirely," Simmons said. "He presented a contested conclusion with more certainty than the evidence justified in a public university classroom."

Rebecca nodded. "Nothing further."

Judge Hayes looked toward David. "Any recross?"

David rose. "One question, Your Honor."

"Proceed."

David looked at Simmons. "Dr. Simmons, would you agree that your objection is not to the discussion itself, but to the level of certainty you believe Professor Price expressed?"

"Yes," Simmons said. "That is accurate."

David returned to his table. "No further questions."

Before stepping down, Dr. Simmons looked briefly toward the jury as Judge Hayes reviewed her notes. "Your Honor, may I clarify one point?"

Judge Hayes looked at both counsel. "Briefly."

Simmons turned back toward the jury. "I disagree with Dr. Monroe's conclusions, but I do not consider them foolish. The origin of life remains one of science's greatest mysteries. Scientists continue to search for answers, and I suspect we will for a very long time."

Judge Hayes thanked Dr. Simmons and excused her from the stand. She then looked toward the clock and announced a fifteen-minute recess. The jurors were escorted out through the side door, and the courtroom released the quiet movement of attorneys gathering papers and reporters preparing notes. Dr. Price leaned toward David while Rebecca organized her files across the aisle. The testimony had not delivered certainty, but it had given both sides admissions they would use later.

"Another honest witness," Price said quietly.

David nodded. "Yes."

"And another disagreement over conclusions."

"Exactly."

Across the room, Rebecca placed Dr. Simmons's outline back into her binder and looked at the next witness list. She believed the defense had preserved its central point: uncertainty was not proof, and mystery was not enough to turn a religious conclusion into academic fact. Still, she could not ignore the concessions. The universe existed, life depended upon astonishingly precise conditions, and DNA carried information no one in the courtroom pretended was simple.

Judge Hayes remained near the bench while counsel prepared for the next stage of testimony. The disagreement, once again, was not over whether the evidence raised serious questions. It was over what explanation the evidence permitted and how far a professor could go when teaching students to weigh those questions. The case was becoming less about slogans and more about categories: evidence, inference, interpretation, and conclusion. That made the trial harder for both sides, and far more useful for the jury.

When court resumed, the testimony would move from biology to something more personal. It would not begin with galaxies, constants, DNA, or cells. It would begin with human beings and the moral judgments they make every day. The next question would be whether right and wrong were merely products of culture and preference, or whether moral law pointed to something beyond humanity itself.

# 7

By the beginning of the second week, the courtroom had settled into a rhythm. The questions surrounding the origin of the universe and the fine-tuning of life had generated countless debates among commentators and scholars, but inside Courtroom One, Judge Eleanor Hayes remained focused on the evidence. The testimony thus far had revealed a recurring theme that neither side could easily avoid. The experts generally agreed on many of the facts. Their disagreements centered on what those facts ultimately meant.

That morning, the testimony would move from the cosmos to the human heart. The jury had heard about beginnings, constants, biological information, and the conditions necessary for life. Now they would hear about right and wrong, and whether morality was merely a human invention or something discovered by human beings across cultures and centuries. Judge Hayes reviewed the witness list, made a note beside the next name, and looked toward the plaintiff's table.

"Mr. Stone," Judge Hayes said. "You may call the plaintiff's next witness."

David rose from the plaintiff's table. "Your Honor, the plaintiff calls Dr. Samuel Whitaker."

A distinguished man in his seventies approached the witness stand with a careful but steady pace. Dr. Samuel Whitaker had spent forty years teaching philosophy and ethics, and his books on morality, justice, and natural law had earned respect among believers, skeptics, and scholars who did not fit neatly into either category. His reputation rested on patience, clarity, and an unusual ability to explain difficult ideas without making them sound smaller than they were. After taking the oath, he waited as the deputy adjusted the microphone. David approached the lectern with a legal pad and a thin folder.

"Dr. Whitaker, does morality exist?" David asked.

"It does."

"What do you mean by morality?"

"The distinction between right and wrong," Whitaker said. "Human beings everywhere recognize certain actions as good and others as evil. They may argue over applications, circumstances, and difficult cases, but the recognition itself is remarkably persistent."

David gave the jury time to write before continuing. "Is that recognition universal?"

"Broadly speaking, yes," Whitaker said. "Cultures differ in application, but certain principles appear throughout history. People condemn murder, praise courage, value honesty, protect children, and seek justice. Even when societies violate those principles, they usually try to justify themselves by appealing to some version of the good."

David turned slightly toward the jury. "Where does that recognition come from?"

"I believe it points to a moral law."

"What do you mean by moral law?"

"A standard that exists above individuals and societies," Whitaker said. "We do not invent it in the same way we invent traffic rules or political procedures. We discover it, argue about it, violate it, and sometimes try to suppress it. The fact that we can judge societies, laws, and customs as unjust suggests that we are appealing to a standard higher than society itself."

David remained near the lectern. "If morality is merely preference, what happens when cultures disagree?"

"Then morality becomes nothing more than power," Whitaker said. "Whoever possesses authority gets to define what is right. History has repeatedly shown us where that leads. If right and wrong are only social preferences, then the strongest society can rename cruelty as order, oppression as policy, and murder as necessity."

"Can you give examples?"

"Slavery, genocide, racism, and human trafficking," Whitaker said. "Entire societies have justified evil and called it good. Some wrote laws to protect it. Some built economies around it. Some educated children to accept it as normal."

David looked toward the jury. "How do we know those societies were wrong?"

Whitaker's expression remained composed. "That is the question. If morality is created entirely by society, then no society can ever be morally wrong in any objective sense. It can only become unpopular later. Yet we all know that certain societies were wrong even when they had public approval, legal authority, and cultural support."

"What does that suggest?"

"That there exists a standard above humanity itself," Whitaker said. "A standard by which individuals, cultures, and governments may all be judged."

David closed his folder. "No further questions."

Judge Hayes looked toward the defense table. "Ms. Kane, you may cross-examine."

Rebecca rose and approached the lectern with a folder marked by several tabs. She gave Dr. Whitaker a courteous nod before opening to the first page. Her voice remained steady, though her questions carried the pressure of someone narrowing a broad argument into a manageable legal point.

"Dr. Whitaker, are you saying atheists cannot live moral lives?" Rebecca asked.

"Not at all."

"Can people who reject belief in God recognize good and evil?"

"Certainly."

"So morality does not require belief in God."

"The recognition of morality does not require belief in God," Whitaker said. "The question is what best explains morality."

Rebecca turned a page. "Societies evolve, do they not?"

"They do."

"And moral standards change over time."

"Societies change in how they understand and apply moral standards," Whitaker said.

Rebecca looked up from the folder. "That sounds like morality evolves."

"Perhaps," Whitaker said. "Or perhaps societies gradually discover where they have been wrong."

Rebecca allowed a brief pause before continuing. "Slavery was accepted in many cultures."

"It was."

"And attitudes changed."

"They did."

"So morality evolved."

"Or people corrected a moral failure," Whitaker replied. "A society can change because it invents a new preference, or because it finally recognizes an old wrong."

Rebecca moved to the next point. "Dr. Whitaker, is morality objective?"

"Yes."

"Can you prove that scientifically?"

"No."

"Can you put morality under a microscope?"

"No."

"Can you measure justice in a laboratory?"

"No."

"So your conclusions are philosophical."

"They are," Whitaker said. "That does not make them unreasonable. Many of the most important truths we rely upon are philosophical before they are practical."

Rebecca closed the folder. "No further questions."

Judge Hayes looked toward David. "Any redirect?"

David rose. "Briefly, Your Honor."

He returned to the lectern. "Dr. Whitaker, Ms. Kane asked whether morality can be proven scientifically. Is science the only path to knowledge?"

"No," Whitaker said. "Science is an extraordinary tool for studying the natural world. It is not the only way human beings know things. Logic, mathematics, moral reasoning, historical inquiry, and legal judgment all involve forms of knowledge that are not placed under a microscope."

David nodded. "Does this courtroom depend on moral assumptions?"

"Yes," Whitaker said. "The oath assumes truthfulness matters. The law assumes justice matters. The jury's task assumes that evidence should be weighed honestly. None of those assumptions can be proven by chemistry, but the courtroom cannot function without them."

David gave a slight nod. "No further questions."

Judge Hayes thanked Dr. Whitaker and excused him from the stand. He stepped down and returned to the gallery without looking toward the reporters in the press section or the faces watching from the public rows. Rebecca reviewed the next witness outline with Mark Ellis before standing again. Judge Hayes looked toward her over the witness list.

"Ms. Kane, you may call the defense's next witness."

"The defense calls Dr. Laura Bennett."

A woman in her early fifties approached the witness stand with the composed confidence of an experienced academic. Dr. Laura Bennett was an evolutionary psychologist and professor at Harvard University. Her work on human behavior, empathy, cooperation, and moral development had earned international recognition, and she had testified before legislative committees on questions involving human behavior and social policy. After taking the oath, she waited for the deputy to adjust the microphone. Rebecca approached the lectern and began.

"Dr. Bennett, does morality exist?" Rebecca asked.

"Absolutely."

"Does morality require God?"

"No."

"Why not?"

"Because morality can be explained through evolution, social development, and human experience," Bennett said. "Human beings survive better when they cooperate. Empathy, fairness, reciprocity, and compassion help communities endure. Over thousands of years, these traits became deeply ingrained in human behavior."

Rebecca nodded. "So morality developed naturally."

"Yes."

"And does a person need religion to recognize right and wrong?"

"No," Bennett said. "People from many religious and nonreligious traditions recognize moral obligations. They may explain those obligations differently, but recognition itself does not require belief in God."

Rebecca glanced toward the jury. "In your opinion, did Professor Price have a right to discuss moral philosophy in his classroom?"

"Yes."

"Did he have a right to present one contested explanation as though it settled the question?"

"No," Bennett said. "A professor may defend a position, but students should understand when a conclusion is debated and when a claim belongs to philosophy, theology, psychology, or social science."

Rebecca returned to the lectern. "No further questions."

Judge Hayes turned toward the plaintiff's table. "Mr. Stone, you may cross-examine."

David approached the lectern with only a few notes. "Good afternoon, Dr. Bennett."

"Good afternoon."

"You believe morality evolved because cooperation benefits survival."

"Correct."

"And evolution explains behavior."

"It explains a great deal of behavior, yes."

David paused briefly. "Does evolution explain why something is wrong?"

"It explains why societies condemn certain actions."

"That was not quite my question," David said. "Does it explain why an action is morally wrong, rather than why a society disapproves of it?"

Bennett considered the distinction. "It explains the development of moral judgment. Whether one calls that objective wrongness enters philosophy."

David nodded. "Is genocide objectively evil?"

"Yes."

"According to what standard?"

"Human dignity," Bennett said.

"And where does human dignity come from?"

"Our shared humanity, our capacity for reason, our vulnerability, our relationships, and our ability to suffer and flourish."

"Why should humanity matter?"

"Because reason and empathy tell us that persons have value," Bennett said.

David did not interrupt. "Would empathy have condemned slavery?"

"Yes."

"What if a society lacked empathy?"

"Then that society would be morally wrong."

"Wrong according to whom?"

Bennett paused. "According to universal moral principles."

David looked down at his notes, then back to the witness. "The very principles we are discussing."

Rebecca rose. "Objection, Your Honor. Argumentative."

Judge Hayes looked toward David. "Sustained. Ask a question, Mr. Stone."

David nodded. "Yes, Your Honor." He returned his attention to Bennett. "Dr. Bennett, where do universal moral principles come from?"

Bennett answered carefully. "There are several accounts. Some philosophers ground them in reason. Some in human flourishing. Some in social contract theory. Some in the nature of persons. I do not believe God is necessary to explain them."

David accepted the answer and moved on. "If morality evolved, then morality helps survival."

"In many cases, yes."

"Does survival tell us what we ought to do?"

"No," Bennett said. "Survival alone does not establish moral obligation."

"Can science fully explain moral obligation?"

"Not fully."

"Can biology fully explain why human beings possess rights?"

"Not entirely."

"Can chemistry explain justice?"

"No."

David allowed the answer to settle. "So when we speak about dignity, justice, rights, and evil, we are speaking about realities that cannot be reduced entirely to chemistry."

"In a sense, yes."

"When you condemn the Holocaust, you are not merely expressing personal dislike."

"No."

"You are saying it was truly wrong."

"Yes."

"Always wrong?"

"Yes."

"Even if an entire society approved it?"

"Yes."

David closed his notes. "No further questions."

Judge Hayes looked toward Rebecca. "Any redirect?"

Rebecca rose. "Briefly, Your Honor."

She returned to the lectern and looked at Bennett. "Dr. Bennett, when you say morality cannot be reduced entirely to chemistry, does that mean morality requires God?"

"No."

"Does acknowledging human dignity require a person to accept religious belief?"

"No."

"Can secular moral philosophy provide serious accounts of rights, justice, and moral obligation?"

"Yes," Bennett said. "Many serious accounts exist, and they deserve careful study."

Rebecca nodded. "Nothing further."

Judge Hayes turned toward David. "Any recross?"

David rose. "One question, Your Honor."

"Proceed."

David looked at Bennett. "Dr. Bennett, would you agree that the existence of serious secular accounts does not prove that Professor Price acted improperly by presenting a theistic account, provided he also allowed opposing views to be examined?"

Bennett paused before answering. "If he framed it as a contested philosophical account and allowed meaningful engagement with opposing views, then presenting it would not be improper simply because it was theistic."

David nodded. "Thank you. No further questions."

Judge Hayes thanked Dr. Bennett and excused her from the stand. The witness left the chair and returned to the gallery with the same composed manner she had shown throughout her testimony. Rebecca made a note in her binder while David returned to his seat beside Professor Price. The exchange had not settled the question of morality, but it had narrowed the issue in a way the jury could understand. The debate was no longer whether human beings recognized good and evil, but what best explained that recognition.

Judge Hayes looked toward the clock and announced a fifteen-minute recess. The jurors were escorted out through the side door, and the courtroom shifted into the quiet movement of attorneys gathering papers and reporters reviewing notes. Professor Price looked toward David as Rebecca closed her folder across the aisle. The morning testimony had not removed the disagreement. It had made the disagreement clearer.

"Another witness who agrees with the facts," Price said quietly.

David placed his notes back into his trial binder. "Yes."

"But not the explanation."

"That is where the case keeps returning."

Across the room, Rebecca reviewed the witness schedule for the following day. She believed Dr. Bennett had protected the defense's central point: morality could be real without requiring the university to treat Professor Price's theistic conclusion as established fact. Still, the testimony had produced concessions she knew David would use. Moral language was unavoidable. Dignity, justice, rights, and evil had entered the record as more than personal taste.

Judge Hayes remained near the bench while the courtroom continued to settle. The testimony had moved from the origin of the universe to life itself and then to morality. Each subject had brought the jury back to the same divide between evidence and interpretation, fact and meaning, recognition and explanation. Yet there remained an objection that had troubled philosophers, theologians, and skeptics for centuries. If God exists, the next question would not be abstract at all.

When court resumed, the testimony would move from moral law to human suffering. The discussion would not begin with galaxies, DNA, or philosophical categories. It would begin with grief, cruelty, disease, and the suffering of the innocent. The next issue would be whether evil disproved God, challenged belief in God, or pointed to the very moral standard both sides had already admitted human beings could not escape.

# 8

BY THE TIME COURT reconvened on Thursday morning, the atmosphere inside Courtroom One had noticeably changed. The previous witnesses had discussed the beginning of the universe, the fine-tuning of life, and the existence of objective moral law. Those subjects, though profound, had remained largely intellectual. Today's subject was different. Every person in the courtroom had experienced suffering in some form, and no one could treat pain as merely an academic category.

Judge Eleanor Hayes entered promptly at nine o'clock and took her seat. The courtroom deputy called the room to order, and everyone sat once the judge gave permission. Judge Hayes reviewed the witness list, then looked toward both counsel tables. David Stone sat beside Professor Daniel Price at the plaintiff's table, while Rebecca Kane reviewed a marked outline at the defense table. The jury watched quietly, aware from the schedule that the morning testimony would address one of the oldest objections to belief in God.

"Good morning," Judge Hayes said. "Counsel, are we ready to proceed?"

"We are, Your Honor," David replied.

"Very well. Mr. Stone, you may call the plaintiff's next witness."

David rose from the plaintiff's table. "Your Honor, the plaintiff calls Dr. Andrew Reynolds."

The witness rose from the front row behind the plaintiff's table and approached the stand. Dr. Andrew Reynolds was sixty-two years old, a professor of philosophy and theology who had spent much of his career studying suffering, evil, and the question of divine goodness. He had written books on the subject, taught at several universities, and participated in public debates with atheists and skeptics around the world. His calm demeanor stood in contrast to the weight of the subject he had come to address. After taking the oath, he waited as the deputy adjusted the microphone.

David approached the lectern. "Dr. Reynolds, many people believe the existence of evil and suffering is the strongest argument against God. Would you agree?"

"I would," Reynolds said.

"Why?"

"Because suffering touches every human being," Reynolds said. "We can discuss cosmology and philosophy academically, but suffering enters our homes. People bury children. Marriages collapse. Disease strikes. Wars destroy families. Every person eventually asks some version of the same question. If God is good, why does evil exist?"

David nodded, letting the answer settle before continuing. "Would you explain that argument to the jury?"

"The argument is fairly simple," Reynolds said. "If God is all-powerful, He could stop evil. If He is all-good, He would want to stop evil. Since evil exists, many conclude that God either lacks power, lacks goodness, or does not exist."

"Does that argument prove God does not exist?"

"No."

"Why not?"

"Because the argument itself assumes something remarkable."

David paused. "What does it assume?"

"It assumes evil is real," Reynolds said.

David remained near the lectern. "Why is that important?"

"Because if evil is real, then good must also be real," Reynolds said. "Evil is not a substance in itself. It is a corruption or violation of what is good. Just as darkness is the absence of light, evil is understood by its relationship to goodness. If objective good exists, then we must ask where that standard comes from."

David looked toward the jury. "So when someone says something is evil, they are doing more than expressing personal dislike."

"Much more," Reynolds said. "They are appealing to a moral standard above themselves. They are saying the world is not as it ought to be. That word ought carries enormous weight."

David turned a page in his notes. "Does Christianity deny the seriousness of suffering?"

"No," Reynolds said. "Christianity takes suffering seriously enough to call evil evil. It does not say pain is imaginary, and it does not tell grieving people that their wounds do not matter. It teaches that the world is morally damaged, that human beings are capable of terrible choices, and that creation itself is not as it was meant to be."

David gave a small nod. "No further questions."

Judge Hayes looked toward the defense table. "Ms. Kane, you may cross-examine."

Rebecca rose and approached the lectern. Her usual confidence was still there, but her movements were slower than they had been with the previous witnesses. She opened her folder and looked at Dr. Reynolds for a moment before asking her first question. The courtroom was quiet enough that the turn of a single page seemed unusually loud. When Rebecca spoke, her voice remained controlled.

"Dr. Reynolds, how would you explain all of this to a mother standing beside the grave of her child?"

The courtroom became silent. Reynolds lowered his eyes briefly, then looked back at her. "Carefully," he said. "And with far fewer words than I would use in a courtroom."

"That was not the answer I expected."

"It is the only honest answer I can give."

Rebecca studied him. "Have you ever had to do that?"

"Yes," Reynolds said. "Twenty years ago, my wife and I buried our only daughter."

Rebecca stopped. Several jurors looked up from their notes.

"She was seventeen," Reynolds continued. "A drunk driver crossed the center line. She died before the ambulance arrived."

Rebecca's expression changed, though only slightly. "I'm sorry."

"So am I," Reynolds said.

Rebecca returned her attention to the folder, though the next question came more quietly. "Did your faith explain it?"

"No."

"No?"

"No," Reynolds said. "I did not receive some special revelation. I still do not understand why it happened."

"Then what good was your faith?"

"It gave me hope when explanations failed."

Rebecca let the answer stand for a moment. "So God allowed your daughter to die and then gave you hope?"

"No," Reynolds said. "We live in a world damaged by sin, human brokenness, and consequences that reach farther than any one person can see. Christianity never promises a world without suffering. It promises redemption in the midst of suffering."

Rebecca picked up a document from the lectern. "Why does God not stop it? If He is all-powerful, why not intervene?"

"Sometimes He does."

"And when He does not?"

"I do not always know why."

"That sounds convenient."

"It is not convenient," Reynolds said. "It is honest."

Rebecca moved to the next question without raising her voice. "What about children with cancer? Earthquakes? Floods? Birth defects? Human free will does not cause all of those things."

"No," Reynolds said. "It does not."

"So why does God allow them?"

"That is one of the hardest questions human beings ask," Reynolds said. "Some suffering comes from human choices. Some comes from living in a fragile, fallen world. Some remains beyond our understanding. Christianity does not answer every why in the way we might want, but it does insist that suffering is not meaningless and that evil will not have the final word."

Rebecca looked toward the jury, then back to the witness. "Isn't it possible that suffering proves God does not exist?"

"Possible as an argument, yes," Reynolds said. "Persuasive to many people, yes. But it raises another question. If there is no God, then on what basis do we call suffering evil in an objective sense?"

Rebecca's eyes narrowed slightly. "Because it harms people."

"Then we must ask why people have objective value," Reynolds said. "Why should the death of a child outrage us? Why should genocide horrify us? Why should injustice matter? If human beings are merely accidental products of blind nature, then pain is biology and death is chemistry. Yet every human heart rebels against that conclusion."

Rebecca did not interrupt him.

"We cry out for justice because we instinctively believe things ought not be this way," Reynolds continued. "We grieve because love recognizes loss as something more than a biological event. We long for a world without death because something inside us tells us we were made for more than death."

Rebecca returned to the lectern. "You understand that many people hear answers like that and still find them inadequate."

"Yes," Reynolds said. "I have been one of them."

"Yet you still believe."

"Yes."

"Why?"

"Because Christianity does not begin with an abstract explanation of suffering," Reynolds said. "It begins with a suffering

Savior. It does not offer a God who remains distant from pain. It offers a God who entered human history, suffered injustice, endured betrayal, experienced grief, and died on a cross. Whatever else someone says about Christianity, they cannot say it presents a God indifferent to human suffering."

Rebecca closed the folder. "No further questions."

Judge Hayes looked toward David. "Any redirect?"

David rose and returned to the lectern. "Briefly, Your Honor."

He looked at Reynolds. "Dr. Reynolds, Ms. Kane asked whether suffering can make belief in God difficult. Can it?"

"Yes," Reynolds said. "Very difficult."

"Can grief make a person angry at God?"

"Yes."

"Does Christianity condemn people simply for asking why?"

"No," Reynolds said. "The Bible is filled with people asking God why. Job asked. David asked. The prophets asked. Jesus Himself cried out from the cross. Honest grief is not the enemy of faith."

David paused. "In your opinion, does the existence of evil remove the question of God, or does it deepen the question?"

"It deepens it," Reynolds said. "If evil is real, then goodness is real. If injustice is real, then justice is real. If suffering should not be, then we are appealing to something beyond personal preference. The problem of evil is a challenge to faith, but it is also a challenge to any worldview that says human beings are nothing more than matter in motion."

David nodded. "No further questions."

Judge Hayes turned toward Rebecca. "Anything further?"

Rebecca remained seated. "Nothing further, Your Honor."

Judge Hayes thanked Dr. Reynolds and excused him from the stand. The witness left the chair and returned to the gallery as the courtroom remained unusually still. The testimony had not answered suffering in a way that could make grief painless, and no one in the room seemed to believe such an answer existed. What it had done was bring the issue into the record without reducing it to slogans. Judge Hayes looked toward the clock and announced a thirty-minute recess.

The jurors were escorted out through the side door, and the courtroom slowly shifted back into movement. Reporters gathered their notes without speaking as loudly as they usually did. David remained seated at the plaintiff's table, reviewing the next witness outline while Professor Price watched Rebecca across the aisle. She sat at the defense table with the same materials in front of her, though for several moments she did not appear to be reading them.

Her mind had returned to another time. She remembered being sixteen years old and sitting in the front row while her father preached on God's faithfulness. She remembered believing every word, because children often trust the voices that shape their world before they learn those voices can break. Then came the affair, the lies, the meetings, the church split, and the divorce. The whispers followed her long after everyone else seemed ready to move on.

She remembered the prayers she prayed during those months. She remembered asking God to fix what adults kept breaking. She remembered the silence she felt when nothing changed. For years, the question had remained beneath her professional discipline and polished arguments. If God exists, why did He not stop it?

Professor Price leaned closer to David while Rebecca gathered herself across the courtroom. "She's angry," he said quietly.

David looked toward the defense table. "No."

Price turned to him. "Then what is it?"

"She's wounded."

Across the room, Rebecca closed the folder in front of her and reached for the witness schedule. Whatever questions she carried, she had no intention of allowing them to affect her performance. She had learned early that composure could protect a person when answers could not. The afternoon witness list sat open before her, and she studied the next name until the room came back into focus. The case was moving again, whether she was ready for it or not.

The trial had moved from science to morality and then to suffering. Now it was about to move into a different arena entirely. The next witness would not speak about galaxies, genetics, philosophy, or pain. He would speak about history, documents, sources, and public facts. Before anyone could debate what Jesus taught, they would have to address a more basic question: whether Jesus of Nazareth actually existed.

# 9

THE AFTERNOON SESSION BEGAN with a different atmosphere than the one that had followed the morning testimony. The discussion about suffering had affected the courtroom in ways statistics, scientific equations, and philosophical categories never could. Some jurors had remained unusually quiet during the recess, and even the reporters in the press section seemed more careful with their voices. In the media room, commentators debated Dr. Reynolds's testimony and argued whether suffering disproved God or revealed humanity's need for redemption. Judge Eleanor Hayes had reminded everyone more than once that emotion was not evidence, and the responsibility of the jury was to consider the facts admitted in court.

When court resumed, Judge Hayes reviewed the afternoon witness list and looked toward the plaintiff's table. The trial had moved from science to morality, and from morality to suffering. Now it would move into history. Before the jury could hear arguments about what Jesus taught, what His followers believed, or what Christianity claimed about Him, they would first have to hear testimony on a more basic question. Did Jesus of Nazareth actually exist?

"Mr. Stone," Judge Hayes said. "You may call the plaintiff's next witness."

David rose from the plaintiff's table. "Your Honor, the plaintiff calls Dr. Jonathan Mercer."

A distinguished man in his early seventies stepped toward the witness stand. Dr. Jonathan Mercer had spent forty years as a historian specializing in ancient Rome and first-century Judaism. He had authored numerous books, lectured at universities around the world, and was considered an authority on historical methodology. Though personally a Christian, his academic reputation had been built on careful scholarship rather than theological argument. After taking the oath, he waited as the deputy adjusted the microphone.

David approached the lectern. "Dr. Mercer, would you briefly tell the jury your field of expertise?"

"I am a historian specializing in the ancient world," Mercer said. "My work focuses particularly on the Roman Empire, Second Temple Judaism, and first-century Palestine."

"How long have you studied those subjects?"

"More than forty years."

David turned slightly toward the jury. "Dr. Mercer, is the existence of Jesus of Nazareth considered a serious matter of debate among historians?"

Mercer gave a restrained smile. "Not among serious historians."

"It is not?"

"No," Mercer said. "The overwhelming majority of scholars, including atheist, agnostic, Jewish, and Christian historians, agree that Jesus of Nazareth existed."

David allowed the answer to settle. "So the historical question is not whether Jesus existed."

"No. The more disputed question is who He was, what He claimed, and what happened after His death."

David nodded. "Why do historians accept His existence?"

"For the same reasons they accept the existence of other figures from antiquity," Mercer said. "We possess multiple sources, both Christian and non-Christian, that refer to Him. Historians examine sources, compare them, test them against what is known from the period, and ask whether the basic claims are historically credible. In the case of Jesus, the evidence for His existence is substantial by ancient standards."

David looked down at his notes. "Could you give examples of those sources?"

"Certainly," Mercer said. "The New Testament documents are historical sources, even though they are also religious texts. Beyond those, we have references in Roman writers such as Tacitus, Jewish sources associated with Josephus, references from Pliny the Younger, Suetonius, and other early materials. These sources support the conclusion that Jesus lived in Judea, was associated with a movement of followers, was crucified under Pontius Pilate, and that His followers soon proclaimed that He had risen from the dead."

Several jurors began writing. David waited before moving to the next question. "Dr. Mercer, are the Gospels considered historical documents?"

"Yes."

"Are they also religious documents?"

"Certainly," Mercer said. "But being religious does not disqualify a document as a historical source. Ancient writers often wrote with purposes, convictions, and perspectives. The question is not whether the author believed something. The question is whether the account contains reliable historical information."

"And what do historians conclude about the Gospels?"

"That they contain substantial historical information," Mercer said. "Scholars debate details, chronology, theological emphasis, and interpretation. Yet the basic existence of Jesus, His public ministry, His crucifixion, and the rise of the early Christian movement are not fringe claims. They are part of the ordinary historical discussion."

David closed his folder. "No further questions."

Judge Hayes looked toward the defense table. "Ms. Kane, you may cross-examine."

Rebecca rose and approached the lectern. She opened a folder marked with several tabs and looked at Dr. Mercer with a calm, professional expression. Her purpose was not to deny what she could not responsibly deny. Her purpose was to narrow the testimony before it expanded beyond what the university believed the evidence could bear.

"Dr. Mercer, the Gospels were written by believers, correct?" Rebecca asked.

"Yes."

"So they have a point of view."

"Of course."

"Would you agree they are biased?"

"Yes," Mercer said. "In the sense that they are written from a perspective."

Rebecca looked up from her folder. "Doesn't bias undermine credibility?"

"No."

"No?"

"No," Mercer said. "Every source contains perspective. The issue is not whether a perspective exists, but whether the testimony is reliable. A biased source may still report accurate information, and an apparently neutral source may still be wrong."

Rebecca moved closer to the jury box but kept her attention on the witness. "Would you agree that eyewitnesses can exaggerate?"

"Certainly."

"They can lie?"

"Yes."

"They can misremember?"

"Yes."

"So why should the Gospels be trusted?"

"That is a fair question," Mercer said. "They were written within the living memory of the events they describe. They include embarrassing details that ancient writers often preferred to omit. They preserve difficult sayings and episodes that were not always convenient for the early church. They contain geographical, cultural, and political details that fit the first-century setting. Also, early opponents of Christianity did not usually argue that Jesus never existed. They argued about who He was and what His followers claimed about Him."

Rebecca turned a page in her folder. "Dr. Mercer, you would agree that extraordinary claims require careful evidence."

"I would."

"The resurrection would qualify as extraordinary."

"Yes."

"Do historians, as historians, prove miracles?"

"Historians evaluate evidence," Mercer said. "Philosophers and theologians often debate whether miracles are possible. A historian can identify facts that require explanation. Whether a miracle is accepted as the best explanation depends partly on the worldview a person brings to the evidence."

Rebecca paused at the lectern. "So history cannot force someone to believe in a miracle."

"No," Mercer said. "History can establish facts that require interpretation."

"Like what?"

"That Jesus existed," Mercer said. "That He was crucified. That His followers believed He rose from the dead. That the Christian movement emerged in the same region where He had been executed. Those are historical facts or conclusions strongly supported by historical evidence."

"But believing something does not make it true."

"Correct."

Rebecca closed the folder. "No further questions."

Judge Hayes looked toward David. "Any redirect?"

David rose and returned to the lectern. "Briefly, Your Honor."

He looked at Mercer. "Dr. Mercer, how does the evidence for Jesus compare with the evidence for other ancient figures?"

"The evidence is very strong," Mercer said. "We have far more manuscript evidence for the New Testament than for many other ancient works. No one doubts the existence of Julius Caesar because his writings and references to him survived through copies. Yet we possess thousands of manuscripts and fragments related to the New Testament tradition, along with multiple early references to Jesus and the movement that followed Him."

"Do historians debate whether Caesar crossed the Rubicon?"

"No."

"Yet we possess fewer sources for many details of Caesar's life than we possess for the early Christian movement."

"That is correct."

David looked toward the jury. "So skepticism about Jesus is usually not about whether He existed."

"No," Mercer said. "It usually concerns His identity, the reliability of particular traditions, and the meaning of the claims made about Him."

David nodded. "No further questions."

Judge Hayes thanked Dr. Mercer and excused him from the stand. The witness stepped down and returned to the gallery while counsel reviewed the next witness list. Rebecca spoke quietly with Mark Ellis before rising again. Judge Hayes looked toward the defense table and waited for the next witness to be called. The afternoon was moving from the existence of Jesus to the reliability of the traditions surrounding Him.

"Ms. Kane," Judge Hayes said. "You may call the defense's next witness."

"The defense calls Dr. Marcus Reed."

A man in his early sixties approached the witness stand. Dr. Marcus Reed was one of the most respected New Testament critics in the world. Though not hostile toward Christianity, he had spent his career arguing that Gospel traditions developed over time and that the church's understanding of Jesus evolved through interpretation, memory, and worship. His books were standard reading in universities across Europe and North America. After taking the oath, he waited for the deputy to adjust the microphone.

Rebecca approached the lectern. "Dr. Reed, do you deny that Jesus of Nazareth existed?"

"No."

"So the question is not His existence."

"No," Reed said. "Serious historians generally agree that Jesus existed."

"What is your concern?"

"My concern is with the reliability and development of some of the traditions surrounding Him," Reed said. "The Gospels were written decades after the events they describe. Oral traditions can develop over time. Stories can be shaped by communities. Religious movements often interpret events through theological lenses."

Rebecca nodded. "So you are not denying history."

"No."

"You are questioning interpretation."

"Precisely," Reed said. "The question is not whether there was a historical Jesus. The question is how much of the later Christian portrait reflects the earliest recoverable history and how much reflects theological development."

Rebecca returned to the lectern. "No further questions."

Judge Hayes looked toward the plaintiff's table. "Mr. Stone, you may cross-examine."

David approached the lectern with a small set of notes. "Good afternoon, Dr. Reed."

"Good afternoon."

"You agree Jesus existed."

"Yes."

"You agree He was crucified."

"Yes."

"You agree His followers believed He rose from the dead."

"Yes."

"You agree Christianity emerged in Jerusalem shortly after His death."

"Yes."

David turned a page in his notes. "Were the disciples in a position to know whether Jesus existed?"

"Of course."

"Were His enemies in a position to deny His existence?"

"Yes."

"Did they?"

"No."

"They accused Him of other things."

"Yes."

"But they did not claim He was imaginary."

"No," Reed said. "That was not the argument."

David moved to the next point. "You testified that traditions can develop over time. Approximately how much time passed before Paul's letters were written?"

"Roughly twenty years after the crucifixion for some of the earliest letters."

"Do those letters present Jesus as a historical figure?"

"They do."

"Do they present Him as crucified?"

"Yes."

"As risen?"

"Yes."

"So belief in the resurrection was not a fourth-century invention."

"No."

"Nor was belief in Jesus' existence."

"No."

David glanced toward the jury before asking the final question. "Dr. Reed, is it fair to say your disagreement with Dr. Mercer is not over whether Jesus existed, but over what the evidence means and how far the evidence can take us?"

"That is fair."

David nodded. "No further questions."

Judge Hayes looked toward Rebecca. "Any redirect?"

Rebecca rose. "Briefly, Your Honor."

She returned to the lectern. "Dr. Reed, when you agree that Jesus existed and was crucified, does that mean you accept every claim made in the Gospels?"

"No."

"Does it mean you accept the resurrection as established history?"

"No."

"What does it mean?"

"It means that certain historical claims are well supported," Reed said. "Other claims require further analysis, and some involve theological interpretation beyond what all historians would accept."

Rebecca nodded. "Nothing further."

Judge Hayes turned toward David. "Any recross?"

David rose. "One question, Your Honor."

"Proceed."

David looked at Reed. "Dr. Reed, would you agree that a conclusion with theological implications is not automatically excluded from historical discussion?"

"Yes," Reed said. "It is not automatically excluded. It simply has to be argued carefully."

David returned to the plaintiff's table. "No further questions."

Judge Hayes thanked Dr. Reed and excused him from the stand. The courtroom remained quiet as he returned to the gallery. David spoke briefly with Nathan Cole before standing again. Judge Hayes looked toward him, and the reporters in the press section began preparing for another witness. The afternoon had already established that the existence of Jesus was not seriously disputed, and the next testimony would move to the documents themselves.

"Mr. Stone," Judge Hayes said. "Do you have another witness this afternoon?"

"Yes, Your Honor. The plaintiff calls Dr. Michael Brennan."

A younger man in his fifties approached the witness stand. Dr. Michael Brennan was a specialist in ancient manuscripts and textual criticism. His work focused on how ancient documents were copied, preserved, compared, and reconstructed from surviving manuscript evidence. He had served on international editorial committees and had spent much of his career examining Greek New Testament manuscripts. After taking the oath, he waited as the deputy adjusted the microphone.

David approached the lectern. "Dr. Brennan, many people assume the Bible has been changed so many times over the centuries that we cannot know what it originally said. Is that accurate?"

"No."

"What do we possess?"

"We possess over five thousand Greek manuscripts and fragments of the New Testament," Brennan said. "We also possess thousands more in Latin and other ancient languages, along with quotations from early Christian writers. The amount of textual evidence is extraordinary by ancient standards."

"What does that evidence tell us?"

"That the New Testament text is remarkably well preserved," Brennan said. "There are textual variants, as there are with any hand-copied ancient work, but the manuscript evidence allows scholars to identify and compare those variants with unusual precision."

David looked toward the jury. "How does that compare with other ancient works?"

"The difference is significant," Brennan said. "Many ancient works survive in a handful of copies, often copied centuries after the originals. The New Testament possesses thousands of manuscripts, many of them much earlier than what we have for other works from antiquity. That does not settle every theological question, but it does mean the text is far better attested than many people assume."

David nodded. "No further questions."

Judge Hayes looked toward the defense table. "Ms. Kane, you may cross-examine."

Rebecca approached the lectern with a narrow binder. "Dr. Brennan, are there differences among the New Testament manuscripts?"

"Yes."

"So errors exist."

"Copying variations exist," Brennan said. "That is true of hand-copied ancient documents generally."

"Some of those variations matter."

"Some are meaningful," Brennan said. "Most are spelling differences, word order, or minor copying variations. A smaller number are more significant, and those are studied carefully."

Rebecca turned a page. "So it would be misleading to tell students there are no variants."

"Yes. That would be misleading."

"It would also be misleading to suggest the manuscript evidence removes every scholarly question."

"Yes," Brennan said. "Textual criticism is a real field because there are real questions to examine."

"But in your opinion, no major Christian doctrine depends on a disputed text."

"That is correct."

Rebecca paused. "That is your view."

"It is the view of many textual scholars," Brennan said.

Rebecca closed the binder. "No further questions."

Judge Hayes looked toward David. "Any redirect?"

David rose. "Briefly."

He returned to the lectern. "Dr. Brennan, do textual variants mean we know less about the New Testament text or more?"

"More," Brennan said. "Because we have so many manuscripts, we can compare them. The abundance of evidence gives scholars the ability to identify where variations occur and evaluate them. A lack of manuscripts would be a much greater problem."

David nodded. "No further questions."

Judge Hayes thanked Dr. Brennan and excused him from the stand. She glanced at the clock, then addressed the jury. The afternoon session had covered more ground than expected, and she saw no reason to force another witness into the remaining time. She reminded the jurors not to discuss the case, not to consume media coverage, and not to form conclusions before all evidence had been presented. Then she recessed court until the following morning.

The deputy called the room to order as Judge Hayes left the bench. David gathered his notes at the plaintiff's table while Professor Price remained seated for a moment, looking toward the empty witness stand. Rebecca placed her materials into her trial binder and spoke quietly with Mark Ellis. The testimony had established that serious historians did not deny Jesus of Nazareth existed. It had also established that the real dispute concerned identity, interpretation, and what conclusions the evidence could reasonably support.

"Good day," Price said quietly.

David looked at him. "A useful day."

"Useful?"

"People do not usually deny Jesus existed," David said. "That was never the hardest part."

Price understood immediately. The historical foundation had been laid, but the next question would be far more contested. It would not ask merely whether Jesus lived or whether ancient documents preserved claims about Him. It would ask what Jesus said about Himself and whether the earliest sources supported those claims. If the evidence showed that Jesus claimed authority beyond that of a teacher, prophet, or reformer, then the case would move into territory neither side could treat as harmless.

Across the courtroom, Rebecca paused before closing her binder. She knew where David intended to go next. The university's defense could concede that Jesus existed, concede that His followers believed extraordinary things, and still argue that Professor Price crossed an academic line by treating those claims as objective truth. The next day would test that line more directly than anything the jury had heard so far. History had established that Jesus lived, and now the question would become who He claimed to be.

# 10

Friday morning brought renewed attention to Courtroom One. Throughout the previous evening, commentators had debated the testimony concerning the historical existence of Jesus. Most agreed that serious historians did not question whether Jesus had lived, and even many skeptics acknowledged that point. The issue that remained was far more controversial. If Jesus existed, the next question was who He claimed to be.

Judge Eleanor Hayes entered the courtroom promptly and took her seat. The courtroom deputy called the room to order, and the jurors were brought in through the side door. Once they were seated, Judge Hayes reviewed the witness list and looked toward both counsel tables. David Stone sat beside Professor Daniel Price at the plaintiff's table, while Rebecca Kane reviewed her notes at the defense table. The room had the quiet pressure of a trial moving toward testimony everyone knew would matter.

"Good morning," Judge Hayes said. "Counsel, are we ready to proceed?"

"We are, Your Honor," David replied.

Judge Hayes looked toward the plaintiff's table. "Mr. Stone, you may call the plaintiff's next witness."

David rose from the plaintiff's table. "Your Honor, the plaintiff calls Dr. Richard Callahan."

A distinguished man in his late sixties rose from the front row behind the plaintiff's table and approached the witness stand. Dr. Richard Callahan had spent forty years studying the New Testament, first-century Judaism, and ancient languages. Though respected among evangelical scholars, he was also known for public debates with skeptics and for his insistence that claims concerning Jesus had to be examined through historical and textual evidence. He had written extensively on the earliest Christian understanding of Jesus and the Jewish background of the Gospels. After taking the oath, he waited while the deputy adjusted the microphone.

David approached the lectern. "Dr. Callahan, throughout history, many people have acknowledged Jesus as a great teacher. Others have viewed Him as a prophet, a moral example, or a religious reformer. Today I want to ask a more specific question. Did Jesus claim to be God?"

"He did," Callahan said.

"Was that claim always stated in a way modern readers immediately recognize?"

"Not always," Callahan said. "Jesus lived and taught in a Jewish culture, and His claims were often expressed through categories His original audience understood better than many modern readers do. He made claims through Scripture, titles, actions, authority, and allusions to Israel's God. Those hearing Him often understood exactly what He meant."

David glanced toward the jury before continuing. "Could you give examples?"

"Certainly," Callahan said. "In John chapter eight, Jesus declared, 'Before Abraham was, I am.' He was not merely claiming to have existed before Abraham. He was using language that echoed the divine name revealed to Moses in Exodus. His audience understood the implication, which is why they responded by attempting to stone Him."

David gave the jurors a moment to write. "Any other examples?"

"In Mark chapter two, Jesus forgave sins," Callahan said. "The religious leaders immediately objected because, in their view, only God could forgive sins in that ultimate sense. Jesus did not correct them by saying they misunderstood Him. Instead, He claimed authority to forgive sins and then connected that authority to His identity as the Son of Man."

David remained near the lectern. "What about John chapter ten?"

"In John chapter ten, Jesus said, 'I and the Father are one,'" Callahan said. "His opponents again took up stones because they understood Him to be making Himself equal with God. Whether someone accepts the claim or rejects it, the narrative presents Jesus as making claims that were far greater than ordinary moral instruction."

David turned a page in his notes. "How does His trial relate to this issue?"

"The high priest asked Jesus whether He was the Messiah, the Son of the Blessed One," Callahan said. "Jesus replied, 'I am, and you will see the Son of Man sitting at the right hand of Power and coming with the clouds of heaven.' That statement combined Psalm 110 and Daniel chapter seven, placing Him in a position of divine authority. The high priest responded by accusing Him of blasphemy."

David looked toward the jury. "So in your opinion, Jesus was not executed merely because He was a teacher."

"No," Callahan said. "He was executed because of who He claimed to be and because those claims were understood as blasphemous by the religious authorities."

David closed his folder. "No further questions."

Judge Hayes looked toward the defense table. "Ms. Kane, you may cross-examine."

Rebecca rose and approached the lectern with a marked folder. She did not challenge Dr. Callahan's credentials, and she did not waste time on issues already conceded by prior witnesses. Her aim was narrower. She wanted to show the jury that interpretation was not the same thing as proof, and that disputed claims about Jesus could not be treated as settled academic fact simply because the plaintiff's experts believed them.

"Dr. Callahan, is it possible that Jesus never actually made some of these claims and that later Christians placed those words in His mouth?"

"That theory has been proposed," Callahan said.

"And do scholars debate that issue?"

"Yes."

"So there is disagreement."

"There is disagreement," Callahan said. "There is also evidence."

Rebecca looked down at her folder. "You would agree that the Gospel of John presents Jesus differently than the Synoptic Gospels."

"It emphasizes different aspects of Jesus' identity and teaching."

"That was not exactly my question," Rebecca said. "John presents a higher and more explicit Christology, correct?"

"More explicit, yes," Callahan said. "I would not say it invented the claim."

Rebecca moved to the next point. "The Gospel of John was written later than Mark."

"Most scholars believe so."

"So later sources present more developed claims."

"Later sources can present claims more explicitly," Callahan said. "That does not mean the claims were invented later."

Rebecca paused at the lectern. "What difficulties do you see with the theory that belief in Jesus' divinity developed over time?"

"Several," Callahan said. "Belief in Jesus' exalted status appears very early. Paul's letters, written within decades of the crucifixion, present Jesus in divine categories. The earliest Christian communities worshiped Him, prayed in His name, and spoke of Him in ways that would have been extraordinary within a Jewish monotheistic context. There is no evidence of a slow movement from ordinary teacher to divine figure over several centuries."

Rebecca looked toward the jury, then back at the witness. "But scholars disagree about how to interpret that evidence."

"Certainly."

"And disagreement means uncertainty."

"Disagreement means disagreement," Callahan said. "Uncertainty depends on the evidence and the question being asked."

Rebecca accepted the answer without reacting. "Dr. Callahan, can you prove mathematically that Jesus claimed to be God?"

"No," Callahan said. "History rarely proves things mathematically. It weighs sources, context, probability, and explanatory power."

Rebecca closed the folder. "No further questions."

Judge Hayes looked toward David. "Any redirect?"

David rose. "Briefly, Your Honor."

He returned to the lectern. "Dr. Callahan, Ms. Kane asked whether scholars disagree. Does disagreement by itself make a conclusion academically improper?"

"No," Callahan said. "If disagreement made a conclusion improper, universities could not teach philosophy, history, ethics, economics, or many areas of science. The issue is whether the conclusion can be supported by evidence and presented with appropriate awareness of opposing views."

David nodded. "Based on your review, is the claim that Jesus understood Himself as possessing divine authority a conclusion that can be argued historically?"

"Yes," Callahan said. "It can be argued historically, textually, and contextually."

David returned to the plaintiff's table. "No further questions."

Judge Hayes thanked Dr. Callahan and excused him from the stand. He stepped down and returned to the gallery while the attorneys reviewed their notes. The testimony had not settled the larger religious question, and no one expected that it would. It had clarified that the dispute was not merely over whether Jesus existed, but whether the earliest evidence supported extraordinary claims about His identity. Rebecca spoke briefly with Mark Ellis before standing again.

"Ms. Kane," Judge Hayes said. "You may call the defense's next witness."

"The defense calls Rabbi Daniel Cohen."

A man in his early seventies approached the witness stand. Rabbi Daniel Cohen had spent decades teaching Jewish history, theology, and Second Temple interpretation. He was highly respected among Jewish scholars and had written widely on messianic expectation, monotheism, and the Jewish context of early Christianity. Though he admired Jesus as a teacher, he rejected Christian claims concerning His divinity. After taking the oath, he waited while the deputy adjusted the microphone.

Rebecca approached the lectern. "Rabbi Cohen, does Judaism regard Jesus as God?"

"No," Cohen said.

"Why not?"

"Because Judaism recognizes God as one and rejects the incarnation," Cohen said. "From a Jewish theological perspective, no human being is to be worshiped as divine. The claim that God became man is not accepted within traditional Judaism."

Rebecca nodded. "Do you believe Jesus claimed to be God?"

"I believe some statements attributed to Him have been interpreted that way by Christians," Cohen said. "I also believe the early Christian movement came to understand Jesus in increasingly exalted terms. From my perspective, those interpretations do not establish that Jesus is divine."

"Do you deny that Jesus was historically significant?"

"No," Cohen said. "He was certainly significant. His movement changed history."

"Do you believe the Christian interpretation of Jesus is required by the historical evidence?"

"No."

Rebecca returned to the lectern. "No further questions."

Judge Hayes turned toward the plaintiff's table. "Mr. Stone, you may cross-examine."

David approached the lectern with a short outline. "Rabbi Cohen, do you believe Jesus existed?"

"Certainly."

"Do you believe He was crucified?"

"Yes."

"Do you believe His followers worshiped Him?"

"They did."

"Do you agree that the charge connected to His execution involved blasphemy before the Jewish authorities?"

"Yes," Cohen said. "That is how the Gospel accounts present it, and the charge fits the conflict described in those sources."

David looked down at his notes. "Whether one accepts His claims or rejects them, would you agree that the claims surrounding Jesus were extraordinary?"

"Yes."

"And His followers believed those claims."

"They did."

"And His opponents objected to those claims."

"Yes."

"So the question is not whether such claims existed."

"No," Cohen said. "The question is how they should be understood and whether they are true."

David gave a small nod. "No further questions."

Judge Hayes looked toward Rebecca. "Any redirect?"

Rebecca rose. "Briefly, Your Honor."

She returned to the lectern. "Rabbi Cohen, when you agree that extraordinary claims surrounded Jesus, are you agreeing that Christianity is true?"

"No," Cohen said. "I am agreeing that Christianity made extraordinary claims. That is a different matter."

"And from your perspective, those claims conflict with Jewish theology."

"Yes."

Rebecca nodded. "Nothing further."

Judge Hayes looked toward David. "Any recross?"

David rose. "One question, Your Honor."

"Proceed."

David looked at Rabbi Cohen. "Rabbi Cohen, would you agree that the fact a claim conflicts with a theological tradition does not mean historians are forbidden from examining the evidence for that claim?"

"Yes," Cohen said. "Historians may examine the evidence. Theology and history often meet at difficult points."

David returned to his seat. "No further questions."

Judge Hayes thanked Rabbi Cohen and excused him from the stand. As he stepped down, Rebecca reviewed her notes and made a mark beside the next witness sequence. The testimony had not settled the issue, and that was exactly what she wanted the jury to understand. It had shown that even serious scholars who accepted Jesus' existence could reject Christian conclusions about His identity. Still, the record now contained another point David would use: the dispute was no longer whether Jesus mattered historically, but whether the claims made by Him and about Him were true.

Judge Hayes glanced toward the clock and addressed the jury. "We will recess for lunch. Members of the jury, remember my instructions. Do not discuss the case with anyone, and do not read, watch, or listen to any coverage concerning these proceedings. We will resume at one-thirty."

The jurors stood and followed the deputy through the side door. The courtroom shifted into the subdued movement of lawyers gathering materials, reporters organizing notes, and spectators waiting for the aisles to clear. David remained seated at the plaintiff's table, reviewing the afternoon witness list. Professor Price watched Rebecca across the courtroom as she placed several documents back into her folder. She moved with her usual discipline, though her expression had become harder to read.

"She looks troubled," Price said quietly.

David did not look away from the defense table. "She is thinking."

"About what?"

"Not merely who Jesus was."

Price looked at him. "Then what?"

David glanced at the witness stand, then back toward Rebecca. "Whether He is who He claimed to be."

Across the courtroom, Rebecca saw the edge of an old photograph partially hidden inside her briefcase. She moved one folder aside and looked at it for only a moment. Her father stood behind a church pulpit with his hand on her shoulder, and she was sixteen years old in a dress she had not wanted to wear. She closed the briefcase before the memory could settle too deeply. There was still an afternoon session ahead, and she had no intention of bringing her past into her cross-examination.

The afternoon would bring the most important testimony of the trial so far. History had established that Jesus lived, and the evidence had suggested that the claims surrounding Him went far beyond moral teaching. The next question would carry even greater weight. It would ask whether the earliest Christian proclamation was grounded in grief, legend, deception, religious experience, or an event in history. If Jesus rose from the dead, the dispute over Professor Price's conclusion would become much harder for the university to contain.

# 11

MONDAY MORNING BROUGHT RENEWED attention to Courtroom One. The previous week's testimony had narrowed the issues considerably. Historians had agreed that Jesus of Nazareth lived, and the testimony concerning His claims had only intensified the debate. Now the trial had reached the central question upon which Christianity itself stood or fell. If Jesus did not rise from the dead, then Professor Price's conclusion would lose its strongest historical foundation.

Judge Eleanor Hayes entered the courtroom promptly at nine o'clock and took her seat. The deputy called the room to order, and the jurors were brought in through the side door. Once they were seated, Judge Hayes reviewed the witness list and looked toward both counsel tables. David Stone sat beside Professor Daniel Price at the plaintiff's table, while Rebecca Kane reviewed her outline at the defense table. The courtroom was quiet in a way that suggested everyone understood the significance of the testimony ahead.

"Good morning," Judge Hayes said. "Counsel, are we ready to proceed?"

"We are, Your Honor," David replied.

Judge Hayes looked toward the plaintiff's table. "Mr. Stone, you may call the plaintiff's next witness."

David rose from the plaintiff's table. "Your Honor, the plaintiff calls Dr. William Grant."

Dr. William Grant, a respected historian and New Testament scholar in his late sixties, approached the witness stand. He had spent decades studying early Christianity, ancient sources, and the historical evidence surrounding the resurrection claim. His books had been used in seminaries and universities, and he was known for arguing that the resurrection should be examined as a historical question rather than dismissed as a religious slogan. After taking the oath, he waited as the deputy adjusted the microphone. David approached the lectern with a legal pad and a marked folder.

"Dr. Grant, does Christianity depend upon the resurrection?" David asked.

"It absolutely does," Grant said. "If Jesus did not rise from the dead, Christianity is false."

David let the directness of the answer settle. "What facts are generally accepted by historians concerning the events surrounding Jesus' death and the rise of Christianity?"

"Jesus died by crucifixion," Grant said. "His disciples sincerely believed they saw Him alive afterward. James, the brother of Jesus, was converted. Saul of Tarsus, who had opposed the early Christian movement, became Paul. Christianity spread rapidly in Jerusalem shortly after the crucifixion. Those facts are accepted by a broad range of scholars, including many who do not believe in the resurrection."

David looked briefly toward the jury. "What about the empty tomb?"

"The empty tomb is accepted by many scholars, though not all," Grant said. "One reason is that the Gospels identify women as the first witnesses. In the first-century world, women were not considered the strongest legal or public witnesses in many settings. If the account had been invented to persuade a skeptical audience, it is unlikely that women would have been placed in that role."

David turned a page in his notes. "What about the creed in First Corinthians fifteen?"

"That creed is extremely important," Grant said. "Paul says he delivered what he had received, that Christ died, was buried, was raised, and appeared to witnesses. Many scholars date that tradition very early, likely within just a few years of the crucifixion. That means belief in the resurrection did not evolve over centuries. It was present at the beginning of the Christian movement."

David remained near the lectern. "So in your opinion, was the resurrection a later invention of the church?"

"No," Grant said. "The evidence shows that the resurrection proclamation was early, central, and foundational."

David closed his folder. "No further questions."

Judge Hayes looked toward the defense table. "Ms. Kane, you may cross-examine."

Rebecca rose and approached the lectern with a narrow binder. She did not rush into the questions, and she did not treat Dr. Grant as an easy witness. Her purpose was to remind the jury that even if early Christians believed something extraordinary, belief and historical certainty were not the same thing. She opened the binder to the first marked page and looked at the witness. Her voice remained steady, though the questions carried the weight of the subject.

"Dr. Grant, extraordinary claims require extraordinary evidence, correct?" Rebecca asked.

"They require sufficient evidence," Grant said.

"The claim that a dead man rose from the dead is extraordinary."

"Yes."

"Can historians prove miracles?"

"No," Grant said. "Historians do not prove miracles in the way a laboratory might prove a repeatable chemical reaction."

"So history cannot prove the resurrection."

"History can establish facts that require explanation," Grant said. "The question is which explanation best accounts for those facts."

Rebecca looked down at the binder. "People hallucinate, do they not?"

"They do."

"People grieve."

"Yes."

"People can sincerely believe things that are false."

"They can."

"Legends develop."

"They do."

"So alternative explanations exist."

"Alternative explanations have been proposed," Grant said.

Rebecca paused, then looked toward the jury. "And because alternative explanations exist, the resurrection is not the only possible explanation."

"It is not the only explanation proposed," Grant said. "In my view, it best accounts for the evidence."

Rebecca closed the binder. "No further questions."

Judge Hayes looked toward David. "Any redirect?"

David rose and returned to the lectern. "Yes, Your Honor."

He looked at Grant. "Dr. Grant, can hallucinations explain an empty tomb?"

"No."

"Can hallucinations explain group appearances to large numbers of people?"

"Not adequately," Grant said. "Hallucinations are private experiences. They do not ordinarily explain multiple people claiming shared appearances in different settings."

"Do legends normally develop within just a few years while eyewitnesses are still alive?"

"Not in the way required here," Grant said. "The early creed is too close to the events to be dismissed as a late legendary development."

"Would the disciples willingly suffer for something they knew to be false?"

"That is highly unlikely," Grant said. "People may die for beliefs that are false, but they do not usually die for claims they personally know they invented."

David nodded. "So while alternative theories exist, each struggles to explain all the facts together."

"Correct," Grant said. "Some theories explain one fact, but fail to account for others. The historical challenge is to find the explanation that accounts for the full body of evidence."

David returned to his table. "No further questions."

Judge Hayes looked toward Rebecca. "Anything further?"

Rebecca rose from the defense table. "Yes, Your Honor."

She returned to the lectern. "Dr. Grant, history cannot place a camera inside the tomb, can it?"

"No."

"And another explanation may someday emerge."

"It could."

"So your conclusion ultimately involves inference."

"As all historical conclusions do," Grant said. "Historians infer the best explanation from available evidence."

Rebecca nodded. "No further questions."

Judge Hayes thanked Dr. Grant and excused him from the stand. He stepped down and returned to the gallery while the courtroom remained unusually attentive. Rebecca spoke quietly with Mark Ellis, then rose again. The defense had conceded many historical points throughout the trial, but she intended to make the line clear. The university did not have to disprove Christianity in order to argue that Professor Price had overstated what academic standards allowed him to present as objective fact.

"Ms. Kane," Judge Hayes said. "You may call the defense's next witness."

"The defense calls Dr. Richard Ellis."

Dr. Richard Ellis, an agnostic historian and author in his early sixties, approached the witness stand. He had written widely on early Christianity and was respected for his cautious approach to miracle claims. Though not hostile toward religion, he had consistently argued that historians should prefer natural explanations when evaluating ancient reports. After taking the oath, he waited for the deputy to adjust the microphone. Rebecca approached the lectern and began.

"Dr. Ellis, do you believe Jesus rose from the dead?" Rebecca asked.

"No."

"Do you deny that His followers believed they saw Him alive after His death?"

"No."

"Do you deny Paul's conversion?"

"No."

"Do you deny the conversion of James, the brother of Jesus?"

"No."

"Do you deny that Christianity spread rapidly in the same region where Jesus had been crucified?"

"No."

Rebecca turned slightly toward the jury. "Then why do you reject the resurrection?"

"Because historians normally work with natural explanations," Ellis said. "Dead people generally remain dead. When evaluating ancient claims, especially miracle claims, historians must exercise caution. Sincere belief does not prove the event happened as interpreted."

Rebecca nodded. "Can sincere people be mistaken?"

"Certainly."

"And extraordinary claims require caution?"

"They do."

Rebecca returned to the lectern. "No further questions."

Judge Hayes looked toward the plaintiff's table. "Mr. Stone, you may cross-examine."

David approached the lectern with a short outline. "Good morning, Dr. Ellis."

"Good morning."

"You agree Jesus died by crucifixion."

"Yes."

"You agree His followers believed they saw Him alive afterward."

"Yes."

"You agree Paul was transformed."

"Yes."

"You agree James was transformed."

"Yes."

"You agree Christianity spread rapidly."

"Yes."

David paused. "So we agree on the central historical facts."

"We do."

"The disagreement concerns the explanation."

"Correct."

David turned a page in his notes. "Can hallucinations explain the empty tomb?"

"No."

"Can legends easily explain the early creed in First Corinthians fifteen?"

"Not easily."

"Could the authorities have ended the movement by producing the body?"

"If they had it and could identify it, that would have been a strong response," Ellis said.

"Did they?"

"Apparently not."

David looked toward the jury, then back to the witness. "Can you provide one natural explanation that accounts for all the facts we have discussed?"

Ellis hesitated. "No. Not one explanation that accounts for all of them equally well."

David gave no visible reaction. "No further questions."

Judge Hayes looked toward Rebecca. "Any redirect?"

Rebecca rose from the defense table. "Yes, Your Honor."

She returned to the lectern. "Dr. Ellis, despite the weaknesses in some alternative explanations, do you believe resurrection is the most probable answer?"

"No."

"Why?"

"Because miracles are extraordinary events," Ellis said. "A historian should be cautious before concluding that a miracle occurred, especially when natural explanations remain possible even if incomplete."

"And history normally deals with ordinary events."

"Correct."

"So caution is appropriate."

"Very much so."

Rebecca nodded. "No further questions."

Judge Hayes looked toward David. "Any recross?"

David rose from the plaintiff's table. "Yes, Your Honor."

David returned to the lectern. "Dr. Ellis, if God exists, would a resurrection be possible?"

"Yes."

"So the question is not whether miracles are impossible."

"No."

"The question is whether the evidence supports one."

"Ultimately, yes."

"And despite rejecting the resurrection, you have admitted that no natural explanation fully accounts for all the evidence."

"That is correct."

David returned to his table. "No further questions."

Judge Hayes looked over her notes, then addressed the witness. "Dr. Ellis, you may step down."

The witness left the stand, and the courtroom remained unusually quiet. Rebecca sat reviewing her notes, though her eyes stayed fixed on the legal pad in front of her. Professor Price leaned slightly toward David while the judge reviewed the witness schedule. The testimony had not forced agreement, but it had placed the central question in sharper focus than anything else in the case. The dispute was no longer whether the resurrection claim existed early. The dispute was whether any explanation could account for the evidence better than the one Christianity had proclaimed from the beginning.

"She's thinking," Price said quietly.

David looked across the aisle. "No."

Price glanced at him. "Then what?"

"She's wrestling."

Judge Hayes looked toward David. "Mr. Stone, does the plaintiff have any additional witnesses?"

David rose. "No, Your Honor. The plaintiff rests."

Judge Hayes made a note and turned toward Rebecca. "Ms. Kane, does the defense have any further witnesses?"

Rebecca rose from the defense table. "No, Your Honor. The defense rests."

Judge Hayes removed her glasses and looked over the courtroom. “Very well. The evidentiary phase of this trial has concluded.”

The words seemed to settle over the room with unusual weight. For nearly three weeks, experts, historians, scientists, philosophers, and skeptics had occupied the witness stand. Questions concerning the origin of the universe, the fine-tuning of life, morality, suffering, history, the identity of Jesus, and the resurrection had been argued from every possible angle. There would be no more testimony. No more exhibits. No more witnesses.

Judge Hayes glanced at the attorneys. “Counsel, are you prepared to proceed with closing arguments tomorrow morning?”

“We are, Your Honor,” David replied.

“We are, Your Honor,” Rebecca answered.

“Very well,” Judge Hayes said. “Court is adjourned until nine o’clock tomorrow morning.”

The deputy called the room to order as Judge Hayes left the bench. As the jurors filed out, neither attorney moved immediately. David remained at the plaintiff’s table while Professor Price sat quietly beside him. Across the aisle, Rebecca began placing documents into her briefcase with more care than speed. The room no longer felt like a place where evidence was being gathered. It felt like a place waiting for judgment.

“That’s it?” Price asked softly.

“For the evidence,” David replied.

“And now?”

David looked across the room toward Rebecca. “Now we trust the jury.”

Across the aisle, Rebecca paused before closing the photograph inside her case. It had remained there throughout the trial, though she had tried not to look at it. She had spent years convincing herself that faith belonged to childhood, that pain had taught her better, and that unanswered prayers were proof enough. Yet over the course of the trial, questions she thought she had buried had quietly returned. She was not ready to admit it, not even to herself, but somewhere beneath the arguments and legal briefs, something was changing.

Tomorrow, no witnesses would testify, and no experts would debate from the witness stand. The attorneys would stand before twelve ordinary men and women and ask them to decide what the evidence meant within the limits of a civil case. The caption still read Price v. Northbridge University, and Judge Hayes would make certain the jury remembered that. Yet everyone in the courtroom understood that the trial had carried questions far larger than the caption. After closing arguments, only one thing would remain: the verdict.

# 12

TUESDAY MORNING ARRIVED WITH a strange quiet that had not existed at any other point during the trial. For nearly three weeks, Courtroom One had been filled with expert witnesses, objections, exhibits, and testimony. Scientists had debated cosmology, philosophers had discussed morality, historians had examined ancient documents, and skeptics and believers had occupied the witness stand. Now the testimony was over, and there would be no more witnesses, no more exhibits, and no more cross-examinations. The evidence had been presented, and the responsibility for weighing it would soon belong to twelve ordinary citizens.

Judge Eleanor Hayes entered promptly at nine o'clock and took her seat. The deputy called the room to order, and the jurors were brought in through the side door. David Stone sat beside Professor Daniel Price at the plaintiff's table, reviewing a closing outline that had been marked and revised until the margins were almost full. Across the aisle, Rebecca Kane read from a narrow folder and then closed it without looking toward the gallery. The courtroom was full, but the silence had the restraint of people who understood that the case had reached its final argument.

Judge Hayes looked toward the jury. "Ladies and gentlemen, you have heard the evidence in this case. What you are about to hear are closing arguments. The arguments of counsel are not evidence. They are intended to help you understand how each side believes the evidence should be interpreted. Your duty is to determine the facts from the testimony and exhibits admitted in court, apply the law as I instruct you, and reach a verdict based only on the evidence."

Several jurors watched the judge closely while others held pens over their notebooks. Judge Hayes continued in the same measured voice. "You must not decide this case based on public opinion, media coverage, personal sympathy, or disagreement with either party's beliefs. This is a civil case between Professor Daniel Price and Northbridge University. The plaintiff has the burden of proof on his claims, and the defendant is entitled to have those claims judged according to the law. With those instructions in mind, Ms. Kane, you may proceed."

Rebecca rose from the defense table and approached the jury. She did not carry the weight of the entire trial in visible emotion, and she did not begin with theatrics. She stood near the lectern, looked at the jurors one by one, and allowed the quiet to do some of the work before she spoke. Her voice was steady, lower than usual, and free from the sharpness she had used during cross-examination. She wanted them to hear reason, not performance.

"Ladies and gentlemen, three weeks ago this case began because Professor Daniel Price stood before students at Northbridge University and presented his conclusions as objective truth," Rebecca said. "No one has questioned his sincerity. No one has questioned his intelligence. No one has questioned his right to believe in God, to practice his faith, or to reach conclusions that matter deeply to him. The issue before you has never been whether faith is permitted. The issue is whether certainty belongs where serious academic dispute remains."

She moved a few steps from the lectern, careful to keep her tone conversational. "You have heard brilliant witnesses during this trial. Some argued for design, and others argued for natural explanations. Some believed morality ultimately points to God, and others disagreed. Some viewed the resurrection as the best explanation of the historical facts, and others remained unconvinced. That range of testimony matters because universities exist in the space where difficult questions are examined, not where one contested conclusion is placed beyond dispute."

Rebecca glanced briefly toward the plaintiff's table, then returned her attention to the jury. "Mr. Stone has repeatedly reminded you that the witnesses from both sides often agreed on certain facts. That much is true. But agreement on facts does not equal agreement on conclusions. Two qualified scientists may agree that the universe had a beginning and disagree about what caused it. Two historians may agree that Jesus existed and disagree about what the evidence proves. Two philosophers may agree that morality matters and disagree about what grounds it."

She returned to the lectern and turned one page in her folder. "Science continues. History continues. Philosophy continues. Questions remain, and throughout human history people have often rushed to certainty before all the evidence was known. Our understanding changes. Knowledge grows. A university must protect the conditions that allow inquiry to continue, including the distinction between evidence, interpretation, and personal conviction."

Rebecca paused long enough for the jurors to write. "The plaintiff wants you to believe that because no alternative explanation answers every question, God becomes the answer. But unanswered questions are not evidence. Possibilities are not proof. Mystery is not a verdict. Intellectual humility requires us to acknowledge what we do not know, even when we feel pressure to settle the matter."

Her voice softened without losing precision. "Professor Price had every right to believe what he believed. He had every right to study these questions, write about them, debate them, and live according to his faith. Northbridge did not discipline him for attending church, reading Scripture, or believing in God. It acted because he presented disputed religious and philosophical conclusions as objective academic truth in a public university classroom. That is the line this case asks you to consider."

Rebecca looked from one juror to the next. "No one is on trial for believing. No one is on trial for praying. No one is on trial for searching for truth. The question is whether Professor Price crossed the line between investigation and dogmatic certainty. When the evidence is weighed carefully, we believe you will find that Northbridge University acted within its responsibility to maintain academic standards. For that reason, we ask you to return a verdict for the defendant."

Rebecca returned to the defense table and took her seat. Judge Hayes made a note, then looked toward the plaintiff's table. David remained still for a moment before rising. Professor Price looked up at him, and David gave the smallest nod before walking toward the jury. He carried a yellow legal pad, though he did not look at it when he began.

"Mr. Stone," Judge Hayes said. "You may proceed."

David stopped near the lectern and faced the jury. "Ladies and gentlemen, Ms. Kane is correct about one important thing. Questions remain. They always will. No scientist understands everything, no historian possesses complete knowledge, and no philosopher answers every mystery. But uncertainty in some areas does not mean uncertainty in every area."

He allowed the sentence to settle before moving on. "For three weeks, you heard testimony from both sides. Scientists disagreed about what caused the universe, but they agreed it had a beginning. Biologists disagreed about design, but they agreed life depends upon astonishingly precise conditions and extraordinary biological information. Philosophers disagreed about the foundation of morality, but they agreed good and evil are real. Historians disagreed over interpretation, but they agreed Jesus lived, was crucified, and that His followers believed He rose from the dead."

David moved a few steps, keeping his pace measured. "The disagreements in this case have not centered on whether the facts matter. They have centered on what best explains those facts. That is not improper in a university classroom. That is precisely what a university classroom is supposed to allow. Professor Price did not shut down inquiry. He invited it. He did not punish disagreement. He encouraged students to test arguments and examine opposing views."

He looked briefly toward Rebecca, then back to the jury. "Northbridge disciplined him because his conclusion pointed toward God. The university says it was protecting academic standards, but the evidence showed something different. Professor Price taught philosophy, ethics, and the history of ideas. Those subjects deal with truth, morality, meaning, human nature, and ultimate questions. A professor in those fields cannot do his work honestly if certain conclusions are ruled out before the evidence is even considered."

David returned near the lectern. "You heard witnesses say that science has limits. You heard witnesses say that morality cannot be reduced entirely to chemistry. You heard historians admit that the resurrection claim was early and central to Christianity. You heard skeptics concede that no natural explanation accounts for all the historical facts equally well. Those admissions did not come from one side only. They came through direct examination, cross-examination, redirect, and recross, under oath and subject to challenge."

He turned a page in his notes but did not read from it. "Professor Price was accused of confusing faith with facts. Yet witness after witness demonstrated that serious faith can be built upon evidence. Historians rely upon evidence. Scientists rely upon evidence. Jurors rely upon evidence. Every day, human beings make responsible decisions by following evidence where it leads, even when every possible question has not been answered."

David's voice remained even. "Professor Price never demanded blind faith. He invited questions. He welcomed criticism. He repeatedly stated that if Christianity were false, no one should believe it. That is not dogmatism. Dogmatism fears scrutiny. Truth invites it."

Several jurors looked up from their notes as David continued. "The defense has asked you to wait for something else. Perhaps another explanation will emerge. Perhaps science will discover something tomorrow. Perhaps historians will uncover a new document. Perhaps philosophy will develop an account that explains morality without God and satisfies every question. Perhaps. But verdicts are not rendered on possibilities. They are rendered on evidence."

He stepped slightly closer to the jury box, though he kept a respectful distance. "If juries waited for perfect knowledge, no verdict would ever be reached. If doctors waited for perfect knowledge, no patient would ever be treated. If scientists waited for perfect knowledge, no hypothesis would ever be proposed. Responsible judgment does not require omniscience. It requires the careful weighing of the evidence available."

David looked toward Professor Price, then back to the jury. "That is what Professor Price did. He examined the evidence available to him. He considered objections. He read the critics. He taught opposing views. Then he reached a conclusion and explained why he believed that conclusion was reasonable. Northbridge did not have to agree with him. It did not have the right to punish him for reaching a reasoned conclusion simply because that conclusion had religious implications."

He returned to the lectern and placed the legal pad down. "This case is not asking you to settle every theological question in human history. It is asking whether a university crossed a legal line when it disciplined a professor for presenting a contested but evidence-based conclusion in a discipline where contested conclusions are the very substance of the work. Professor Price followed the evidence where he believed it led. The evidence in this courtroom shows that he did so honestly, carefully, and within the proper bounds of academic inquiry."

David paused before the final portion of his closing. "At the beginning of this trial, Ms. Kane told you this case was about truth. She was right. Truth is not threatened by questions. Truth is not weakened by examination. Truth does not need the protection of institutional fear. When the evidence is complete, and now it is complete, we ask you to find that Northbridge University crossed the line from academic oversight into unlawful punishment."

He gave the jury a respectful nod and returned to the plaintiff's table. Judge Hayes waited until he was seated before turning back to Rebecca. "Ms. Kane, you may proceed with rebuttal."

Rebecca rose again. The courtroom remained silent as she approached the jury box more slowly than before. Her face showed no anger, and when she spoke, her voice carried the controlled exhaustion of a lawyer who knew the final words mattered. She did not open with an attack. She looked at the jurors as people who had been asked to carry an unusually difficult responsibility.

"Ladies and gentlemen, Mr. Stone says verdicts are based on evidence, and he is right," Rebecca said. "But evidence and conclusions are not the same thing. The witnesses agreed on many facts. Intelligent men and women then reached very different conclusions from those facts. That matters because this case is not about whether Professor Price may think deeply.

It is about whether he presented disputed conclusions with a certainty the evidence did not justify in that classroom."

She turned slightly toward Professor Price. "I do not believe Professor Price acted maliciously. I believe he acted sincerely. I believe he cares about his students, his work, and the questions he spent his life studying. But honest people can be wrong. Sincere people can overstate their conclusions. A good motive does not automatically make an academic judgment proper."

Rebecca returned her attention to the jury. "The plaintiff has repeatedly spoken of what best explains the evidence. That phrase sounds careful, and sometimes it is. But there is a difference between offering an explanation and presenting certainty. There is a difference between saying, 'Here is a contested conclusion I believe the evidence supports,' and saying, 'This is objective truth and the matter is settled.' That difference is where Northbridge University had a responsibility to act."

She paused, allowing the courtroom to settle around the point. "No witness came into this courtroom claiming to possess all the answers. No witness claimed there were no mysteries. No witness proved God. What you heard were arguments, interpretations, inferences, and competing frameworks. Those things belong in the university, but they must be identified honestly. Students deserve the difference between evidence and interpretation."

Her tone softened. "Questions concerning God have occupied humanity for thousands of years. Great minds have disagreed. They still do. Perhaps they always will. That does not make faith worthless, and it does not make Professor Price a bad man. It simply means a university may insist that contested claims be presented with proper academic humility."

Rebecca looked toward the jurors one last time. "This case is not about whether Professor Price is sincere. He is. It is not about whether faith has value. It does. It is not about whether people should search for truth. They should. It is about whether a public university may require a professor to distinguish between evidence, interpretation, and certainty. The evidence shows that Northbridge acted reasonably, and the defense asks you to return a verdict in its favor."

Rebecca returned to counsel table and sat. Judge Hayes looked down at her notes, then removed her glasses and addressed the jury. The room was completely still. Outside the courthouse, the crowds were still waiting, the commentators were still speaking, and the country was still arguing. Inside the courtroom, only twelve people mattered now.

"Ladies and gentlemen, tomorrow morning I will instruct you on the law," Judge Hayes said. "After those instructions, the case will be yours for deliberation. You are not to discuss the case until I formally submit it to you. You are not to read, watch, or listen to any media coverage, and you are not to form or express a final opinion until you have heard all of my instructions and begun deliberations with your fellow jurors."

The deputy called the room to order as Judge Hayes left the bench. The jurors were escorted through the side door, and neither counsel table moved for several moments. David looked down at his notes, then closed the folder in front of him. Professor Price sat beside him in silence, as though the absence of testimony had made the room feel larger. Across the aisle, Rebecca placed her closing outline into her briefcase and sat with her eyes fixed on the polished surface of the table.

The arguments were finished. There would be no more witnesses to rescue either side from what had already been said. The next morning, Judge Hayes would instruct the jury on the law, and then twelve ordinary citizens would decide the case that had drawn the attention of the nation. The caption still read Price v. Northbridge University, but the trial had carried questions far older than any civil docket. Tomorrow, those questions would follow the jurors into the deliberation room.

# 13

THE BAILIFF CLOSED THE door behind the twelve jurors and left them alone for the first time since Judge Eleanor Hayes had delivered her instructions. For three weeks they had sat together in Courtroom One, listening to experts, lawyers, and witnesses discuss questions that stretched far beyond the issue that had brought them there. They had heard testimony about the beginning of the universe, the complexity of life, morality, suffering, history, and the resurrection of Jesus Christ. Millions had followed the case from outside the courthouse, but none of that mattered inside the jury room. The cameras, reporters, commentators, and spectators were gone, and the responsibility now rested with twelve ordinary people seated around a long table.

Frank Dawson sat near the end of the room with the verdict forms placed in front of him. After forty years as an aerospace engineer, he had learned to solve problems by separating facts from assumptions, and the past three weeks had given him more than enough of both. Beside him sat Maria Alvarez, a high school history teacher and widow who had filled three notebooks during the trial. Across from her sat Leonard Shaw, a construction contractor whose strong opinions and stubborn personality had made him one of the most outspoken jurors. Denise Walker, an oncology nurse who had spent decades caring for cancer patients, sat quietly beside him, her notes arranged in careful order.

Paul Jensen, a software engineer and outspoken atheist, occupied a seat near the end of the table with two legal pads covered in small, precise handwriting. Sheila Morrison, a retired principal and lifelong Christian, sat beside him with a copy of the jury instructions open in front of her. Anthony Russo, who owned a restaurant with his brothers, leaned back in his chair and looked as though he would rather face a dinner rush than another hour of legal discussion. Evelyn Brooks, a retired librarian, sat near the window and watched the others before speaking. Marcus Reed, a homicide detective, had arranged his notes with the same precision he used when preparing cases, while Patricia Nguyen, an accountant, had highlighted pages in different colors. Harold Bennett, a retired Army colonel, sat upright near the corner, and Rebecca Collins, the youngest juror, listened with the guarded attention of someone still deciding where she fit in the room.

Frank placed the verdict forms in the center of the table. "I do not think we should vote yet," he said. "I would rather hear what everyone thinks before we start counting sides."

No one objected. A few jurors looked relieved, and several reached for their notes as if the decision not to vote had given them permission to breathe. The judge's instructions sat on the table between them, printed, stapled, and more complicated than any headline outside the courthouse had suggested. This was not God versus the university, despite what people had been shouting for weeks. The caption was still Price v. Northbridge University, and the question was whether the university had unlawfully punished Professor Price for protected academic expression.

Leonard was the first to speak. "I'll save everybody some time. I think the university had a point. Professors should not be teaching religion as fact."

Harold looked up from the instructions. "That is not exactly what Judge Hayes asked us to decide."

Leonard shook his head. "That is what everyone keeps saying, but I do not buy it. If Price's conclusions were unreasonable, then the university had every right to step in."

Paul looked over from his notes. "I do not think that is what happened."

Leonard gave him a surprised look. "Coming from you, that is interesting."

"What does that mean?" Paul asked.

"It means you told us during jury selection you were an atheist. I figured you would be sitting beside me on this."

Paul gave a faint smile. "I probably would have three weeks ago."

Anthony looked across the table. "Three weeks ago?"

"I am still an atheist, Anthony. Relax."

The room loosened enough for a few quiet laughs. Anthony shook his head and looked toward the ceiling for a moment. "I do not know what I am. I just know I do not trust religion."

Harold turned toward him. "You said something like that during lunch one day."

Anthony nodded. "My brother spent years in Catholic school. One of the priests abused him. He never got over it.

Drugs, drinking, therapy, the whole thing. He is alive, but the guy I grew up with disappeared years ago."

No one interrupted him. The room had been filled with arguments about God, reason, morality, and evidence, but Anthony's words brought the discussion down to one family and one wounded man. He did not look at anyone while he spoke. "So if I sound angry at religion, maybe I earned it."

Harold nodded quietly. "I am sorry."

Anthony looked down at the table. "Sorry does not fix him."

"No," Harold said. "It does not."

Frank waited before speaking again. "I think that is exactly why Judge Hayes warned us about personal experience. None of us came into this room empty. We all brought something with us. We need to be honest about that without letting it replace the evidence."

Marcus nodded. "That is the job."

Maria looked around the table. "Then maybe we should start with what we are actually deciding. Not whether Christianity is true in some absolute sense. Not whether everyone agrees with Professor Price. The issue is whether Northbridge crossed the line when it disciplined him."

Patricia turned to the jury instructions. "The judge said we have to decide whether his speech was protected academic expression and whether the university's stated reason was legitimate or pretextual. That is more specific than what people outside are arguing about."

Leonard leaned back. "Fine. But if his speech was irresponsible, then the university had a legitimate reason."

Paul tapped his pen against his notes once, then stopped. "Maybe. But we heard testimony that he presented opposing views. We heard students were allowed to disagree. We heard no evidence that he punished anyone for rejecting his conclusions."

Denise spoke for the first time. "And we heard the university wanted him to call his conclusions personal belief rather than reasoned conclusions. That bothered me."

Leonard looked at her. "Why?"

"Because I spend my life around suffering," Denise said. "Patients believe all kinds of things when they are dying. Some are religious. Some are not. I know belief can be emotional, but that does not mean every belief is irrational. The university seemed to assume that if the conclusion pointed toward God, it had to be downgraded automatically."

Sheila looked toward Frank. "I think we should go through the witnesses one at a time. Not to retry the whole case, but to see what the record actually showed."

Frank nodded. "That was my thought. No vote yet. We talk through the evidence and then decide where everyone stands."

Rebecca Collins gave a nervous smile. "Like twelve angry people?"

Anthony laughed. "More like twelve tired people."

The room relaxed again, and even Leonard smiled despite himself. Paul flipped through his notes while Evelyn checked the page numbers in her notebook. They had heard fourteen witnesses and enough testimony to fill a library. Some of it had been technical, some emotional, and some difficult to place within a civil verdict form. The challenge was not whether they had heard enough words. The challenge was deciding which words mattered legally.

Frank looked around the table. "Before we start, does anyone already know where they stand?"

Six hands rose, though not with the confidence Frank expected. Five favored Professor Price. One favored Northbridge University. The remaining six stayed undecided, and Frank noticed that most of the undecided jurors were the ones who had taken the most notes. Leonard looked around the room and let out a short breath.

"Really?" Leonard said. "Only one with me?"

Anthony lifted one hand halfway. "Not exactly. I am undecided."

"So am I," Paul said.

Denise nodded. "Same."

Harold glanced toward Leonard. "I do not think that means anyone has won the room."

Leonard looked at the verdict forms, then back at Frank. "Fine. Let's hear the evidence."

Sheila turned to the first page of her notes. "I think we should remember something before we start. Nobody on that witness stand claimed to know everything."

Marcus nodded. "That stood out to me too. The honest witnesses made the case harder, not easier."

"Even the experts disagreed," Rebecca Collins said.

Maria looked at her notes. "Mostly over interpretation."

Patricia added, "Not always over facts."

Frank pointed his pen toward Patricia. "That may be where we begin. The facts everyone agreed on, then what conclusions were presented, then whether Price was allowed to present his conclusion in a philosophy class."

Leonard looked unconvinced. "And if we decide Price was wrong?"

Marcus answered without hesitation. "Being wrong is not misconduct."

Leonard turned toward him. "Then what is?"

"Silencing debate. Punishing disagreement. Misrepresenting what happened. Applying rules differently because administrators disliked the conclusion."

Anthony smiled slightly. "Detective answer."

Marcus looked at him. "Occupational hazard."

Evelyn spoke quietly, and the room turned toward her because she had said very little during the trial. "I spent thirty-five years as a librarian. People always think libraries are quiet because nobody is arguing. That is not true. Libraries are full of arguments. The whole point is that the arguments are allowed to sit on the same shelf."

Maria smiled at that. "That may be the best description of a university I have heard in three weeks."

Leonard leaned forward. "But universities also have standards."

"They do," Evelyn said. "The question is whether the standard was applied fairly."

Frank picked up one of the yellow legal pads. "Then we start with the first major area: cosmology. Carter and Pierce agreed the universe had a beginning. They disagreed on the explanation."

Anthony looked at the clock. "Are we really starting with the origin of the universe before lunch?"

Frank glanced toward the coffee pot near the side table. "Not before coffee."

That brought another round of quiet laughter, and for the first time since entering the jury room, the tension eased in a way that felt useful rather than careless. They were not ready to vote, and no one pretended they were. The verdict forms remained untouched in the center of the table, while the jurors gathered their notes and began preparing to work through the evidence. Outside the room, the courthouse waited. Inside, the first real deliberation was about to begin.

None of them realized yet how difficult the process would become. Before they reached a verdict, each person around the table would confront questions that extended beyond the courtroom and into old wounds, old beliefs, and assumptions they had carried for years. Some would defend convictions they had never before been forced to explain. Others would discover that issues they thought had been settled long ago were not settled at all. Somewhere between the evidence, the law, and their own experiences, twelve strangers would begin the difficult work of separating truth from assumption.

# 14

THE FOLLOWING MORNING, THE twelve jurors filed back into the deliberation room carrying coffee, legal pads, and the lingering uncertainty none of them had expected to feel after three weeks of testimony. The previous afternoon had accomplished little beyond convincing them that no quick vote would settle the matter. Frank Dawson was content with that. During his years as an aerospace engineer, he had learned that difficult questions were rarely solved by impatience. They were solved by breaking problems into smaller pieces and examining them carefully.

After everyone settled into their seats, Frank looked around the room. The verdict forms remained in the center of the table, untouched since the day before. He had no interest in forcing a vote before the jurors had worked through the evidence in a disciplined way. The judge's instructions still governed the room, and Frank wanted everyone to remember that they were not there to decide whether God existed. They were there to decide whether Northbridge University had unlawfully punished Professor Daniel Price for protected academic expression.

"I think we ought to start where the testimony started," Frank said. "Dr. Benjamin Carter and Dr. Alan Pierce. Let's talk through what they actually said before we decide whether Professor Price's position was unreasonable."

Maria Alvarez opened her notebook. Over the course of the trial, she had recorded nearly every exchange between witnesses and attorneys. Years of teaching high school history had trained her to listen for what people agreed on before getting lost in what they argued about. She looked around the table, then turned to the first section of her notes. Several jurors waited while she found the page she wanted.

"The interesting thing about those two men," Maria began, "is that they agreed on far more than I realized at first. Both testified that the universe had a beginning. Neither one denied that space, time, matter, and energy came into existence in connection with that beginning. The disagreement was not over whether the evidence mattered. It was over what the evidence meant."

Leonard Shaw shook his head. "That is because Carter stepped outside science."

Denise Walker looked over at him. "Did he?"

"Of course he did," Leonard said. "Talking about God is not science."

"He did not quote the Bible," Denise said. "He was not talking about Christianity during that testimony. He was talking about causes."

Leonard gave a dismissive shrug. "Same difference."

"No, I do not think it is," Maria replied. "He did not say science proved God. He said science points beyond itself. That is not the same claim."

Anthony Russo took a sip of coffee and leaned back in his chair. "I liked Pierce better."

"So did I," Leonard said.

Anthony nodded. "He seemed more comfortable saying, 'I do not know.'"

Paul Jensen had been looking through his notes while the others spoke. He finally looked up, and the room quieted because most of them had learned that Paul did not speak unless he had already worked through the point in his head. "Actually, Carter said that too."

Anthony smiled. "You defending the plaintiff now?"

Paul laughed under his breath. "No. Believe me, nobody is more surprised than I am."

The room loosened with quiet laughter, and even Leonard allowed a small smile. Paul turned back to his notes and tapped the page with his pen. "I am serious. I expected Carter to sound like a preacher in a lab coat, but that is not what I heard. He admitted science could not prove God mathematically. Pierce admitted science could not explain why anything exists at all. They both admitted there were unanswered questions."

Patricia Nguyen nodded as she reviewed her highlighted notes. "And Stone got Pierce to admit that the multiverse remains theoretical."

Leonard frowned. "That does not mean it is not true."

"No," Patricia agreed. "It means Carter was not irrational for disagreeing with it."

Marcus Reed leaned forward, his notes arranged in the same careful order he had kept since deliberations began. "I kept thinking about my work. Witnesses disagree all the time. Detectives disagree. Prosecutors disagree. Defense attorneys disagree. Facts can remain the same while explanations vary, and that does not automatically make someone dishonest."

Frank gave a faint smile. "Engineers are the same way."

Everyone looked toward him.

"You would be surprised how many arguments happen in design meetings," Frank said. "People fight over theories, methods, models, and what the data means. Sometimes one person is right and the other is wrong. Sometimes both are partly right and both are missing something. Nobody gets fired simply because they interpret difficult data differently."

Anthony grinned. "Maybe they should put engineers in Congress."

"Not a chance," Frank replied.

The room laughed, and the sound eased some of the pressure that had gathered around the table. Rebecca Collins had been listening quietly from her seat near the end, her notebook open but mostly blank for that section. She looked from Frank to Maria, then toward Paul. Her voice was careful, as though she was still deciding whether the question sounded foolish.

"Can I ask something?"

Frank nodded. "Go ahead."

"If Carter and Pierce agreed the universe had a beginning, why did the news make it sound like they were complete opposites?"

Maria smiled. "Because disagreement sells better."

Paul nodded. "And because people do not always hear nuance."

Rebecca looked down at her notes. "I thought Carter was going to say science proved God."

"So did I," Anthony admitted.

"But he never did."

"No," Paul said. "That is what surprised me."

Leonard leaned back in his chair. "I still think science will answer those questions eventually."

Harold Bennett looked toward him. "Maybe."

Leonard narrowed his eyes slightly. "That is not much of an answer."

"No," Harold said. "But neither is pretending we know things we do not know. That is what impressed me about both witnesses. Neither one claimed certainty."

Anthony glanced at him. "You think Carter was not certain?"

"I think he was convinced," Harold said. "There is a difference."

"What difference?"

"A convinced man can still admit his limitations," Harold said. "When I was in the Army, I served under officers who disagreed constantly. Good men. Smart men. They would look at the same intelligence reports and come away with different conclusions. Nobody accused the other of being crazy just because they disagreed. They argued, tested assumptions, and made the best decision they could with the information they had."

Leonard studied him for a moment. "You believe in God."

"I do."

"Then you are biased."

Harold gave him a patient look. "Maybe. Carter had beliefs. Pierce had beliefs. You have beliefs. So do I. Everybody comes to evidence with assumptions, which is why the way they handled disagreement mattered to me."

Leonard did not answer right away. Harold continued, not pressing but not backing away either. "I did not see two men trying to destroy each other. I saw two intelligent scientists wrestling with the same evidence. Pierce rejected Carter's conclusion, but he did not call him irrational. That matters in a case about whether a professor should be punished for reaching a contested conclusion."

Marcus nodded. "That is exactly what I saw."

"So did I," Denise said.

Leonard looked around the room. "Am I the only one who thinks Pierce was closer to the truth?"

"No," Anthony said. "I agree with you."

Leonard looked relieved. "Finally."

"But I do not think Carter was irrational."

The relief left Leonard's face. Anthony lifted one shoulder, more tired than argumentative. "I do not buy Carter's conclusion, but he seemed honest. If the question is whether Price was allowed to discuss that kind of reasoning in a philosophy class, I am not sure the university wins just because I disagree with him."

Evelyn Brooks, who had remained quiet for most of the morning, finally spoke. Her voice was soft, but the room turned toward her because she had a way of making silence feel intentional rather than empty. "I think honesty was what impressed me most."

Frank looked toward her. "What do you mean?"

"I spent years telling myself that science had replaced God," Evelyn said. "After my husband died, I did not want anything to do with religion. I never hated God. I just stopped thinking about Him, because thinking about Him made the grief harder."

No one interrupted her. Denise looked at her with the recognition of someone who had sat beside too many hospital beds to treat grief as an argument. Evelyn took a moment before continuing. "Listening to Carter and Pierce reminded me of something I had forgotten. Scientists do not know everything. That does not make science weak. It may simply mean honest people know where their knowledge ends."

"No one knows everything," Denise said quietly.

Evelyn nodded. "Exactly. Maybe admitting that is not weakness. Maybe it is humility."

Paul looked down at his legal pad. "I walked into this trial convinced that belief in God was intellectual surrender. I thought people believed because they were afraid of not having answers."

Anthony looked at him. "And now?"

Paul smiled. "I am not becoming a Christian before lunch, if that is what you are asking."

The room laughed again, and Paul waited until it passed. "I still do not believe. But I do not think Carter was afraid. I do not think Pierce was afraid either. I think both men followed the evidence as they understood it. That is different from what I expected."

Frank closed his notebook and looked around the table. "Maybe that is the point."

Nobody spoke. The room had reached one of those pauses that felt less like confusion and more like recognition. The jurors were not agreeing about God, science, or the beginning of the universe. They were agreeing about the narrower question

Judge Hayes had placed before them. Frank looked toward the verdict forms, then back to the others.

"We are not deciding who is right about the origin of the universe," he said. "We are deciding whether Professor Price was unreasonable, dishonest, or outside the bounds of academic inquiry for believing what he believed and presenting the evidence as he understood it."

Leonard stared at the table. "I still think Carter is wrong."

"No problem there," Harold said.

"And I think Pierce is closer to the truth."

"That is your right."

Leonard let out a long breath. "But I cannot honestly say Carter was irrational."

Frank nodded. "Neither could Pierce."

That observation seemed to settle over the room. Nobody had changed his or her worldview in any simple way. Harold still believed in God. Paul still considered himself an atheist, though perhaps with less certainty than before. Anthony remained suspicious of religion, and Leonard remained unconvinced by Carter's conclusions. Yet by the time they broke for lunch, the jurors had reached one point of agreement.

Dr. Benjamin Carter and Dr. Alan Pierce had looked at the same universe and reached different conclusions. Neither man had accused the other of dishonesty. Neither had called the other irrational. Both had acknowledged unanswered questions, and both had defended their positions without pretending the other side had nothing to say. The jurors wrote that point on the board under the heading Frank had created: **Cosmology — Facts and Disputed Inferences.**

As Frank gathered his notes, he found himself wondering whether that fact said something important about Professor Price. If respected scientists could disagree without demanding each other's silence, perhaps disagreement itself was not enough to justify punishment. That did not decide the case, and Frank knew better than to pretend it did. It only gave them a place to begin. For the first time since deliberations started, beginning felt possible.

# 15

The jurors returned from lunch with less tension than they had felt the day before. Their discussion about Dr. Benjamin Carter and Dr. Alan Pierce had not changed anyone's beliefs, but it had changed the tone of the room. They had begun to understand that disagreement itself was not evidence of misconduct. Frank Dawson suggested they continue moving through the witnesses in the order they had appeared. No one objected, and Maria Alvarez opened her notebook to the next section.

"Next up is Dr. Elizabeth Monroe and Dr. Karen Simmons," Maria said.

Anthony Russo smiled. "The DNA witnesses."

"Basically," Maria replied. "Monroe argued that the information contained in DNA points to intelligence. Simmons argued that future discoveries may provide a natural explanation."

Leonard Shaw leaned back in his chair. "And I thought Simmons got the better of that argument."

Patricia Nguyen looked up from her notes. "Maybe. But she also admitted there are things we still do not understand."

"Of course there are," Leonard replied. "That is how science works."

Paul Jensen nodded as he reviewed the page in front of him. "I actually appreciated Simmons."

Anthony laughed. "You appreciated everybody."

Paul smiled, though he kept his eyes on the notes. "No. Seriously. I expected her to dismiss Monroe completely. Instead, she admitted there are unanswered questions. She disagreed with Monroe, but she did not pretend Monroe was stupid."

Denise Walker looked across the table. "She impressed me too. She was not defensive."

"Neither was Monroe," Harold Bennett added. "I thought both women were careful."

Rebecca Collins flipped through her notes, then looked around the room. "Can I ask something?"

Frank gave her a small smile. "You do not need permission."

Rebecca laughed quietly, then turned back to the page she had marked. "I kept hearing the word information. Monroe said DNA contains information. Simmons agreed. But neither one seemed to give a complete answer for where that information came from."

Patricia nodded. "That is exactly what I noticed."

Leonard frowned. "Maybe we just have not figured it out yet."

"Maybe," Marcus Reed said. "But that is not an explanation. That is a possibility."

Leonard shrugged. "Science has solved a lot of mysteries."

"It has," Marcus agreed. "But solving one mystery does not automatically solve another."

Paul looked down at his legal pad. "What surprised me was Stone's question."

Denise turned toward him. "Which one?"

"When he asked Simmons whether information is different from complexity," Paul said. "A snowflake can be complex, but it does not contain coded instructions. DNA does. Simmons agreed with that distinction."

Anthony nodded. "I remember that."

Paul continued. "She also admitted we do not currently possess a complete explanation for abiogenesis. She did not say science had solved it. She said scientists continue searching."

Maria flipped through her notes and found the line. "I wrote that down too. She said there is no complete explanation for the origin of genetic information."

Harold nodded. "Which was honest."

Leonard looked at him with irritation that was more tired than angry. "You keep saying that."

"Because honesty matters."

Leonard let out a breath. "You know what bothers me? Every time science does not know something, religious people act like they have scored a point."

Harold shook his head. "I do not think Monroe did that."

"No?"

"No," Harold said. "She was not saying, 'We do not know, therefore God.' She argued that information is something we consistently trace back to intelligence. You may disagree with that inference, but it is not the same as filling a gap with religion."

Anthony rubbed his chin. "I actually thought she made a decent point."

Everyone looked at him.

"What?" Anthony asked.

Leonard stared at him. "You?"

Anthony laughed. "Relax. I am not joining a monastery."

The room laughed, and Anthony waited until it passed. "I am serious. My restaurant has computers, recipes, inventory systems, schedules, vendor records, and payroll. Information always comes from somebody. When Monroe talked about DNA containing instructions, that made more sense to me than I expected."

Paul smiled. "That is close to what Monroe argued."

"And Simmons did not really answer it," Anthony said.

Patricia adjusted her glasses. "She answered it differently. She said future discoveries may explain it."

Frank leaned forward. "Which means the disagreement was not over the existence of DNA."

"No," Maria agreed. "It was over what DNA means."

Evelyn Brooks, who had spent much of the morning listening quietly, looked up from her notebook. "When I worked at the library, people used to bring in books that had been damaged. Sometimes pages were missing. Sometimes they were out of order. Sometimes the binding had come loose and sections were scattered. No one ever questioned whether books came from authors."

Denise smiled. "That is an interesting comparison."

Evelyn nodded. "I am not saying DNA is exactly like a book. I am saying information always seemed to point somewhere. Even when information is damaged or incomplete, we still recognize it as information."

Leonard shook his head. "That is where I get off the train. You are making assumptions."

"So are scientists," Paul said.

Leonard turned toward him. "Now you are defending Monroe."

"No," Paul said. "I am defending consistency. We all make assumptions. Simmons assumed natural explanations will eventually account for the evidence. Monroe assumed information is best explained by intelligence. Both were making inferences."

Marcus nodded. "In investigations, we do the same thing. Evidence points somewhere. Then we argue about where."

Frank gave a faint smile. "That is engineering too."

"And accounting," Patricia added.

"And medicine," Denise said.

Anthony laughed. "So everybody's profession agrees with God?"

"No," Denise replied. "Everybody's profession interprets evidence."

That observation quieted the room. The jurors were beginning to recognize a pattern that had not been obvious when they were sitting in the courtroom listening to testimony in real time. The experts had not divided into smart people and foolish people, or honest people and dishonest people. They had divided over how far the evidence could take them. The distinction mattered because the case was not asking them to declare which worldview had won the debate.

Harold looked across the table. "You know what struck me about both witnesses? Neither one tried to embarrass the other. Simmons respected Monroe. Monroe respected Simmons.

They disagreed, but neither acted like the other woman had no right to be in the conversation."

Leonard nodded reluctantly. "I will give them that."

"And that is what bothers me about Northbridge," Harold continued. "Price was not inventing ideas nobody else held. Monroe's views are shared by respected scientists and scholars. You may disagree with them, but you cannot pretend they are irrational."

Leonard stared at the table for several moments. "I still think Simmons is right."

"No problem there," Frank said.

"And I think one day science will explain it."

Paul smiled. "Maybe."

Leonard looked at him. "Do not start sounding like Harold."

Paul shook his head. "I am not. But I have noticed something."

"What?"

"Every witness on both sides keeps admitting they do not know everything."

Denise smiled. "That is called being human."

"And maybe that is why I trusted them," Paul said. "Nobody claimed perfect certainty. The honest ones kept telling us where knowledge ended and inference began."

Maria closed her notebook halfway, leaving her finger inside the page. "I think that is what we have seen so far. Carter and Pierce. Monroe and Simmons. Smart people. Honest people. Different conclusions."

Frank nodded. "And Price lost his career because he agreed with one side."

The room became quiet. That sentence moved the discussion back to the verdict form in the center of the table. They were not there to decide whether Leonard was right about future science, whether Harold was right about God, or whether Paul would leave the trial with the same confidence he had carried into it. They were there to decide whether the university had acted lawfully when it disciplined a professor for teaching a conclusion that other serious scholars were willing to defend.

Nobody had changed their beliefs in any simple way. Leonard remained convinced that natural explanations would eventually prevail. Harold still believed the evidence pointed toward God. Anthony still distrusted religion, even while admitting Monroe had made a point he could understand. Paul still called himself an atheist, though the word no longer sounded as settled in his own mind. By the time they prepared to move on to the next witnesses, they had reached another point of agreement.

Dr. Elizabeth Monroe and Dr. Karen Simmons had examined the same evidence and reached different conclusions. Neither woman had accused the other of dishonesty, and neither had treated disagreement as misconduct. Simmons had challenged design, Monroe had challenged naturalism, and both had acknowledged that essential questions remained unanswered. Frank wrote the point on the board beneath the previous heading: **Biology — Information, Complexity, and Competing Inferences.**

He capped the marker and looked back at the table. "Reasonable people disagree," he said.

No one argued with that. It was becoming a familiar theme, and with every witness they discussed, the jurors found themselves less concerned with who had won each argument and more concerned with whether Professor Price had done anything deserving punishment. So far, none of them had seen it. That did not end the deliberations, but it changed the burden of the conversation. The evidence was beginning to move the room.

# 16

FRANK DAWSON'S YELLOW LEGAL pad remained in the center of the table, angled slightly toward Maria, with the words reasonable disagreement written near the top in his squared engineer's handwriting. No one had asked him to write it down, and no one had voted on it. Yet after their discussion of Dr. Carter and Dr. Pierce, the phrase seemed to belong there. It had become the first solid point the twelve jurors had managed to agree upon. They were not deciding which worldview was true, but whether Professor Daniel Price had stepped outside the boundaries of honest academic inquiry.

The deliberation room had changed since they first entered it. The nervous formality of twelve strangers locked together by civic duty had begun to wear thin. Coffee cups had shifted from one side of the table to the other, and legal pads were filled with arrows, question marks, witness names, and private observations written in the margins. They were still careful with one another, but they were no longer merely being polite. They had begun to listen.

Maria Alvarez turned a page in her notebook and stopped when she saw the next pair of names. Dr. Samuel Whitaker. Dr. Laura Bennett. She remembered the shift that had happened in the courtroom when the testimony moved from science to morality. The beginning of the universe had felt vast and distant, something too large to touch. DNA had felt intricate and mysterious, but still safely contained within expert language. Morality was different because morality did not remain on the witness stand. It followed people into memory, conscience, regret, anger, and grief.

Maria looked up from her notes. "The next witnesses were Whitaker and Bennett. This was the testimony on the moral law."

Leonard Shaw leaned back in his chair and rubbed one hand over his jaw. He had been restless through most of the morning, but now his discomfort seemed less like combativeness and more like irritation at being cornered by a question he could not easily dismiss. "That one bothered me. Not because Whitaker sounded foolish. He did not. That is what bothered me. He asked questions that sounded simple until you actually tried to answer them."

Sheila Morrison watched him with the steady patience of a retired principal who had spent years listening to frustrated parents, frightened children, and tired teachers. She did not answer as if she were correcting him. She spoke slowly, giving him room to hear her. "What part bothered you most?"

"I do not need religion to tell me murder is wrong," Leonard said. "I do not like the idea that if I believe evil is real, then I am somehow borrowing from God."

Sheila nodded. "I do not think Whitaker said you need religion to know murder is wrong. I wrote that down because I had the same concern at first. He made a distinction between recognizing morality and explaining morality. His argument was not that atheists cannot be moral. His argument was that if morality is objective, if some things are truly right or wrong regardless of opinion, then there has to be a foundation beneath that moral law."

Paul Jensen sat beside her with his pen balanced between two fingers. He had entered the jury room with the posture of a man who trusted clean logic more than emotional claims, but the trial had begun to unsettle the categories he had brought with him. "That is what I heard too. If Whitaker had argued that nonbelievers cannot be moral, I would have dismissed him. But he did not say that."

Frank looked toward Paul. "How did you understand his point?"

Paul glanced at his notes. "He was asking why morality has authority over us. Why do we say something is wrong even when it benefits someone? Why do we condemn an action even if a society approves it? I did not like the question, but I understood it."

Anthony Russo gave a tired laugh and shook his head. His chair creaked as he shifted his weight. "I still think people make morality too complicated. You do not kill people. You do not steal from people. You do not abuse children. You do not betray your family. You do not need a philosopher to explain that. My mother could have told you all of that while stirring sauce on a Sunday afternoon."

A few of the jurors smiled, but Marcus Reed did not. He had been reading through his notes from Whitaker's testimony, and his years as a detective had made him suspicious of easy answers when the subject was evil. "You do not need a philosopher to know it. But knowing something and explaining it are not the same thing."

Anthony looked toward him. "What do you mean?"

"I have interviewed men who could explain every step that led to a murder," Marcus said. "They could tell me what they felt, what they wanted, what they feared, and why they thought they had no choice. Some sounded rational. Some even sounded sorry. But explanation never made the act right. That was the part of Whitaker's testimony I could not shake. Motive explains behavior. It does not excuse it."

Patricia Nguyen adjusted the cap on her highlighter and turned one of her pages toward Frank. Her notes were organized more cleanly than anyone else's, with different colors for direct testimony, cross-examination, and admissions made by the witnesses. "Dr. Bennett's testimony made sense to me on one level. Cooperation helps communities survive. Empathy helps people live together. Fairness reduces conflict. Moral rules can develop because societies need order. I understood her argument."

Frank waited, because Patricia sounded as though she had more to say.

"But I kept writing the same thing in the margin," Patricia continued. "Useful is not the same as right."

Frank nodded. "That is an important distinction."

"It is," Patricia said. "Something can be useful and still be wrong. A government can use fear to control people. A company can use dishonesty to increase profits. A person can use manipulation to get what they want. Those things may work, but that does not make them good."

Maria nodded. She had taught history long enough to know that some of humanity's darkest chapters had been defended with intelligent arguments and protected by law. "That is why Whitaker's examples were strong. Slavery was legal. Segregation was legal. Governments have committed atrocities under the authority of law. If morality comes only from society, then society cannot truly be wrong. It can only be different from another society."

Leonard stared at the table. He had an answer for almost everything, but this question held him longer than the others. "I understand the point. I just do not like where it goes. Religious people hear that and immediately say, therefore God. That is what bothers me. They take a hard question and use it as a doorway to preach."

Harold Bennett had been listening without reacting as if Leonard's comment offended him. If anything, he seemed to appreciate the honesty. "Some people do that. But I do not think Whitaker did. He was careful. He was saying that if moral obligation is real, then morality must be grounded in something deeper than human preference. You do not have to agree with his conclusion to admit the question is serious."

Anthony's expression changed, and some of the humor left his face. "My problem is that religious people talk about morality like they own it. I have seen too many people do wicked things while quoting Scripture. My brother was hurt by a man who wore a collar and talked about God. So when somebody tells me morality points to God, I have a hard time not hearing hypocrisy."

The room grew quieter, but it was not the kind of silence that belonged in a movie. It was the silence of people deciding not to rush past a wound. They had heard pieces of Anthony's story before, but each time he mentioned his brother, the conversation changed. His anger no longer sounded like an argument. It sounded like grief that had learned to defend itself.

Harold waited before answering. When he spoke, his voice was softer than before. "What happened to your brother was evil. Not unfortunate. Not merely painful. Evil. The fact that a religious man did it does not make it less evil. It makes the hypocrisy worse."

Anthony looked down at the table. "That is easy to say."

"I know," Harold said. "But the only reason we can call it hypocrisy is because there is a standard higher than that man's title, position, and words. He claimed one thing and lived another. That gap is what we are judging."

Anthony did not argue, but he did not fully agree either. The conversation moved on because everyone seemed to understand that some answers needed more time than a deliberation room could give. Denise Walker spoke next, and her years as an oncology nurse gave her words a different kind of authority. She had seen suffering up close, not in textbooks or court transcripts, but in hospital rooms where families whispered prayers, doctors lowered their voices, and machines kept rhythm beside bedsides.

"In medicine, survival is not the same as goodness," Denise said. "Cancer survives. Disease spreads. A tumor can grow aggressively and take over a body. If all we mean by morality is survival, nature gives us some terrible examples. I have watched people die who were more loving, more honest, and more selfless than people who lived. Survival alone cannot define what is good."

Paul rested his pen on his notebook and stared at the page without writing. "That was what bothered me during Dr. Bennett's testimony. Her explanation made sense when she talked about cooperation and social development. But when Stone asked whether evolution could explain what we ought to do, she admitted it could not fully answer that."

Frank looked toward him. "You agreed with that?"

"As a software engineer, yes," Paul said. "I can design a system that rewards cooperation. That does not make the system moral. It only means the system functions a certain way."

Rebecca Collins had been quiet for several minutes. She was the youngest juror and had no strong religious background to defend or reject. That made her questions simpler than some of the others, but often sharper. "So the question is whether morality is something humans invented or something humans discovered."

Maria smiled faintly. "That is one way to frame it."

Rebecca looked from Maria to the others. "Did we create right and wrong because it helped us survive, or did we slowly learn to recognize something that was already real? I do not know what I believe about God, but when Whitaker asked whether genocide would still be wrong if an entire society approved it, I knew my answer. It would still be wrong. I do not know how to explain that without saying there is something above society."

Leonard looked at Rebecca, then at Harold. "That still does not prove God."

Harold answered without hesitation, but without pressing the point too hard. "Not by itself. But it makes Price's argument reasonable, and that is the issue before us."

Frank wrote slowly on the legal pad beneath the words already there. Moral foundation disputed. He did not underline it, circle it, or call for agreement. He simply left it where everyone could see it. The phrase was not a verdict, but it captured the point they kept returning to. The witnesses had not disagreed over whether human beings recognize morality. They had disagreed over what morality is grounded in.

Evelyn Brooks, who had spent much of the afternoon listening, looked toward the center of the table. "After my husband died, I stopped going to church. I did not become an atheist exactly. I just stopped wanting answers from God. But I never stopped believing that some things should not happen."

No one interrupted her. Evelyn rarely spoke for long, but when she did, her words carried the quiet gravity of someone who had lived with grief instead of merely studying it.

"When someone is betrayed, when a child is harmed, when someone suffers cruelty, people do not usually say it was merely inconvenient or biologically unfortunate," Evelyn continued. "They say it was wrong. I think Whitaker's testimony reminded me that even anger assumes the world ought to be different than it is."

Leonard exhaled and rubbed his forehead. "I still think Bennett gave the more realistic explanation. People learn right and wrong from family, culture, consequences, empathy, and experience. That is how life works. But I admit Whitaker exposed a problem. If a whole society approves something evil, I still want to say that society is wrong, not just different. I do not like the problem, but I see it."

Paul looked at him with a small smile. "That may be the most honest thing you have said since we came in here."

Leonard gave him a tired look. "Do not get used to it."

The room loosened with a few quiet laughs, and the tension eased without disappearing. Frank looked around the table. "What I keep hearing is the same pattern we noticed with the scientists. Whitaker and Bennett did not disagree over whether people recognize morality. They disagreed over what morality is grounded in. Bennett gave a natural explanation for how moral behavior could develop. Whitaker argued that moral obligation requires something higher than human preference."

Marcus nodded. "And neither one said Price had no right to raise the issue."

Patricia looked again at her notes. "That is important. The university treated his conclusion like misconduct. But this is a real debate. Serious people disagree over it."

Anthony leaned back and looked toward the ceiling. "I still do not trust religion. I do not know if I ever will. But I cannot say Whitaker was making a stupid argument."

Sheila's expression softened. "He was not. And admitting that does not require you to agree with everything he believes."

Paul closed his notebook halfway, then opened it again as if he was not ready to be finished with the thought. "I came into this trial thinking arguments for God were mostly emotional. I thought people believed because they needed comfort or because they were afraid of uncertainty. But this argument was not emotional the way I expected. It was uncomfortable because it pressed on something everyone already knows. If good and evil are real, then reality may be bigger than chemistry."

Frank looked down at his legal pad again. He had not meant for his notes to become a record of the jury's slow movement, but that was what they were becoming. Reasonable disagreement. Moral foundation disputed. The phrases were not verdicts, but they mattered. They showed that Professor Price had not stepped into shallow water. He had stepped into one of the oldest and most difficult debates in human history.

By the time they finished discussing Dr. Whitaker and Dr. Bennett, no one in the room claimed to have solved the question of morality. Leonard still leaned toward Bennett's natural explanation. Harold and Sheila believed Whitaker had pointed toward God. Anthony remained guarded. Paul remained unsettled. Denise, Maria, Patricia, Marcus, Evelyn, Rebecca, and Frank all recognized that the testimony had raised serious questions that could not be dismissed with slogans.

Leonard looked at the words on Frank's pad and sat silently for a long moment. Then, with visible reluctance, he said what several of them had been circling around all afternoon. "If the moral argument belongs in this jury room, it is hard to argue it had no place in a classroom."

Frank did not underline the statement or call for a vote. He simply wrote one more note beneath the others and set the pen down. The issue was not settled, but it was serious. That was enough for the moment. With every witness they reviewed, the room was moving farther from the noise outside the courthouse and closer to the question Judge Hayes had actually placed before them.

# 17

FRANK'S FINAL NOTE FROM the moral law discussion remained on the yellow pad longer than anyone expected. The issue was not settled, but it was serious. The sentence seemed to belong not only to morality, but to everything they had reviewed so far. The beginning of the universe had been serious. The design of life had been serious. The question of right and wrong had been serious. None of those discussions had produced certainty in the room, but each had made it harder to dismiss Professor Daniel Price as reckless or irrational.

Maria Alvarez turned to the next page in her notebook and hesitated before reading the witness names aloud. She remembered the way the courtroom had changed during that testimony. The air had become heavier, and even the attorneys had seemed less combative for a while. Suffering was not merely another argument to be won. It was the one question every person carried in some form, whether they admitted it or not.

"The next witnesses were Dr. Andrew Reynolds and Dr. Thomas Avery," Maria said. "That was the testimony about evil and suffering."

No one responded immediately. The earlier discussions had been difficult, but this one was different. The jurors could debate cosmology, biology, and morality with some distance. They could discuss the beginning of the universe without remembering a hospital room. They could discuss DNA without seeing a grave. Suffering had a way of refusing to stay theoretical.

Denise Walker set her pen down. She had been a nurse long enough to recognize the shift in the room before anyone named it. People sat differently when the subject was pain. They looked at the table, stopped making jokes, and became careful with their voices. She had seen the same thing countless times when doctors walked into rooms with test results.

"I thought Reynolds was the strongest witness emotionally," Anthony Russo said. "But I do not know if that means he was the strongest witness logically. Losing his daughter was terrible. I do not think anyone in that courtroom was not moved by it. Pain does not prove God."

Sheila Morrison nodded slowly, accepting the point without surrendering the issue. "No, pain does not prove God. That was not exactly his argument. He said suffering raises the hardest question against God, but it also raises a question for every worldview. If evil is real, then good must be real. If something is truly wrong, then there has to be a standard beyond personal preference."

Leonard Shaw leaned back in his chair. His voice carried less aggression than before, but more resistance. "That is where I think he was clever. He took the hardest argument against God and turned it around. I do not deny evil is real. I just do not see how that helps the case for God. If anything, evil makes belief in God harder."

Paul Jensen had been staring at the notes in front of him for several minutes. His page from Reynolds's testimony had fewer technical phrases than the earlier ones. Instead, he had written questions in the margins. Why justice? Why outrage? Why should not be? He tapped the page once with his pen, then stopped.

"I agree that evil makes belief in God harder," Paul said. "But Avery admitted something that bothered me. When Stone asked him what ultimate meaning suffering has if there is no God, Avery said none. No final justice. No ultimate hope. No redemption. I appreciated his honesty, but I did not like the answer."

Anthony turned toward him. "Because it is bleak?"

"Because it does not match how we actually live," Paul said. "When something horrible happens, nobody really talks as if it is just chemistry and biology. Even people who do not believe in God talk like the world is broken, like something has gone wrong. That is not proof of God, but it made me realize atheism does not get to avoid the problem of suffering. It just answers it differently."

Marcus Reed looked across the table. As a homicide detective, he had learned to hide his reactions, but the topic of final justice cut closer to his work than he wanted to admit. "I have sat with families after murders. Some of them never saw a conviction. Sometimes the suspect was known but the evidence was not enough. Sometimes the case went cold. Sometimes a jury did not believe the right witness."

The room stayed quiet while Marcus continued. "When people say they want justice, they do not mean they want a better coping mechanism. They mean they want the wrong made right. I do not know what that proves about God, but I know this much. The desire for justice runs deeper than survival."

Patricia Nguyen studied the two pages where she had separated Avery's testimony from Reynolds's testimony. The categories no longer seemed as clean as they had during the trial. "Avery was not weak," she said. "I thought he gave the strongest answer for Northbridge. He did not mock faith. He did not pretend suffering was simple. He said the existence of innocent suffering makes belief in an all-powerful and loving God highly difficult. That is a serious argument."

Harold Bennett nodded. "It is."

Patricia looked at him, almost surprised by the agreement. "Then how do you answer it?"

Harold did not answer right away. He looked down at the table, the silence around him carrying the weight of memory rather than hesitation. When he finally spoke, his voice was calm but not casual. "I do not answer it easily. I have buried friends. I have watched men die who were better than I was. I have stood beside families when there was nothing useful to say."

He paused, and no one pushed him. "I do not believe faith gives us permission to pretend suffering is small. Reynolds did not pretend that. He said Christianity does not begin with an explanation of suffering. It begins with a suffering Savior. That matters to me because it means God is not presented as distant from pain."

Leonard's expression tightened. "But it still does not explain why God does not stop it."

"No," Harold said. "It does not explain every why."

"Then what good is it?"

"It gives hope where explanation ends."

The answer echoed Reynolds's testimony, but Harold did not say it like a quotation. He said it like something learned the hard way. Evelyn Brooks looked at the tabletop, her eyes fixed somewhere beyond the wood grain. When she spoke, her voice was gentle, but it carried more strength than anyone expected.

"When my husband died, people tried to explain it to me," Evelyn said. "Some said God needed him. Some said everything happens for a reason. Some said I would understand someday. I know most of them meant well, but none of it helped. It made me angry. It made me feel like my grief was a theological problem they were trying to solve."

Denise looked toward Evelyn but did not interrupt. The room allowed the silence to remain because everyone seemed to understand that some memories needed space before they could be spoken. Evelyn continued without raising her voice.

"What I appreciated about Reynolds was that he did not pretend he understood why his daughter died. He said he did not know. That was the first honest answer I had heard in this trial about suffering. He did not offer an explanation wrapped in religious language. He said his faith gave him hope when explanations failed."

Anthony looked down. "Hope is good. But hope does not undo what happened."

"No," Evelyn said. "It does not."

The simplicity of her answer settled over the table. It did not feel like a dramatic moment. It felt like twelve people recognizing that some losses could not be repaired by winning an argument. Rebecca Collins, who had listened quietly through most of the discussion, spoke with hesitation.

"I do not have a story like some of you," Rebecca said. "I mean, I have lost people, but not like that. What confused me was that Avery and Reynolds both seemed honest. Avery said suffering makes God hard to believe in. Reynolds said suffering makes atheism hard to live with. I do not know which one is right, but I believed both of them when they said the question was difficult."

Maria looked back at her notes from the cross-examinations. "That may be the important part. Neither witness gave an easy answer. Avery admitted atheism has no ultimate justice. Reynolds admitted Christianity does not explain every instance of suffering. Both were honest about the cost of their worldview."

Leonard shook his head, though there was weariness in it now. "I still think suffering is the strongest argument against God. I do not care how many ways people explain it. Children get cancer. Innocent people die. Predators hurt people and hide behind religion. Families pray and nothing changes. If God is there, He seems absent too often."

Anthony stared at him for a moment, recognizing a familiar anger. "You sound like you know what that feels like."

Leonard's jaw tightened. For a moment, it seemed he might snap back, but he did not. He looked toward the closed door as if deciding whether to keep something locked away.

"My father was a church man," Leonard said. "Sunday morning, Sunday night, Wednesday night. He carried a Bible with notes in the margins and could quote more verses than any pastor I ever heard. People at church thought he was a godly man."

No one interrupted him.

"At home, he was mean," Leonard continued. "Not all the time. That was the worst part. Some days he was fine. Other days he came home angry, or drunk, or both, and everybody in the house learned to disappear. My mother covered bruises with makeup and still made sure our shirts were ironed for church. I sat in a pew every week listening to men talk about love while wondering why God did not see our house."

The words did not come out as a speech. They came unevenly, with long pauses between thoughts, as though Leonard had not planned to say any of it. The jurors listened without offering the kind of comfort that would have sounded too small for what he had just given them.

"So when people tell me God is good, I do not hear theology," Leonard said. "I hear my father singing hymns with the same hands he used to put holes in doors."

The room remained still. Harold's expression changed, but he did not try to answer quickly. Sheila looked at Leonard with the quiet sorrow of someone who had seen too many children shaped by homes no one suspected. Anthony looked away first, perhaps because Leonard's anger now sounded too much like his own.

Harold finally spoke. "I am sorry. What your father did was evil. The fact that he used religion makes it worse, not better."

Leonard gave a bitter smile. "That is what Christians always say when one of their own turns out rotten."

"Maybe," Harold said. "But I am not trying to protect him. I am saying he violated the very God he claimed to worship. His hypocrisy does not prove God is evil. It proves your father was."

Leonard's eyes hardened again. "Convenient."

"No," Harold said. "Painful. There is nothing convenient about saying a man can sit in church and still be wicked. But if we judge your father as wicked, then we are already appealing to a standard higher than him. Higher than the church that admired him. Higher than the image he managed to protect."

Paul watched Leonard carefully. Something in the exchange seemed to bring together the moral law discussion and the problem of evil in a way no witness had managed to do from the stand. "That is what bothers me," Paul said. "I do not want to believe in God just because I need justice. But I also do not know what to do with the fact that I need justice."

Patricia looked at him. "What do you mean?"

"If there is no God, then Leonard's father may have fooled the church, hurt his family, died, and gotten away with it," Paul said. "That is not just emotionally unsatisfying. It feels wrong at a level I cannot explain."

Patricia added quietly, "Avery would say that feeling is human, but not ultimate."

"Exactly," Paul said. "And maybe he is right. But I do not like what that means."

Frank had not written anything for several minutes. He had set his pen down and listened as the conversation moved from argument to confession. The deliberation room no longer felt like a place where experts were being evaluated. It felt as though the testimony had found its way into the lives of the people charged with judging it.

Denise looked toward Leonard. “I have watched people pray and still die. I have watched good families suffer and cruel people go home healthy. I do not have a neat answer for that. But I also know that when I held the hand of a dying child, I never once thought her life was just biology. I never thought her suffering was meaningless. Something in me rejected that before I had words for it.”

Leonard’s face softened slightly, though he said nothing. Maria turned back to the legal question, not because she wanted to avoid the pain in the room, but because the pain needed somewhere to land.

“So what did Reynolds and Avery show us about Professor Price?” Maria asked. “Avery showed that suffering is a serious objection to belief in God. Reynolds showed that Christianity has a serious response, even if it does not answer every why. Neither witness was shallow. Neither mocked the other. They both treated the question with weight.”

Marcus nodded. “And Avery admitted suffering creates a problem for atheism too. No ultimate justice. No final reckoning. No redemption. That matters.”

Anthony rubbed his hands together and sighed. “I still do not like religious answers to suffering. I have heard too many bad ones. But Reynolds was not giving the kind of answer I hate. He was not saying pain is not real. He was not saying people should just get over it. He said Christianity gives hope because God entered suffering. I do not know if I believe that, but I understand why people do.”

Sheila looked briefly toward Leonard before returning to the group. "And Price never claimed suffering was simple. He claimed faith could be defended even in the face of suffering. That is not the same as pretending suffering does not matter."

Frank picked up his pen again. Beneath the earlier notes, he wrote slowly enough for the others to see the words forming.

Suffering unresolved, but not ignored.

He looked at the phrase for a moment, then set the pen down. No one objected. The words did not answer the problem of evil, and Frank knew they were not meant to. They simply recorded what the jurors had learned from the testimony. The question was not shallow, and Professor Price had not treated it as shallow.

By the end of the discussion, no one had solved the problem of evil. Leonard had not surrendered his anger. Anthony had not lost his suspicion. Evelyn still carried grief. Denise still carried the faces of patients she had watched suffer. Paul remained unsettled by the thought that a world without God might also be a world without final justice. Harold and Sheila remained convinced that Christian hope was not an escape from suffering, but an answer within it.

What had become clear was that Professor Price had not avoided the hardest question. He had faced it, and the witnesses on both sides had treated it as worthy of serious thought. If suffering made belief difficult, it also made unbelief costly. The jurors did not all agree on what that meant, but they could no longer pretend the question belonged only in churches or private grief.

Frank looked once more at the yellow pad. Reasonable disagreement. Moral foundation disputed. Suffering unresolved, but not ignored. The notes were beginning to look less like fragments and more like a map of the trial itself. For the first time since deliberations began, Leonard did not argue when Frank left the pad in the center of the table.

# 18

MARIA ALVAREZ HAD BEEN waiting for this part of the discussion more than she wanted to admit. The earlier subjects had stretched her, especially the testimony about science and suffering, but history was familiar ground. She had spent twenty-six years teaching students how to handle old documents, partial records, biased sources, political motives, and gaps in the evidence. Ancient history was never as clean as people wanted it to be, but it was not guesswork either. Historians worked with fragments, and from those fragments they reconstructed lives, events, movements, and empires.

She turned to the next section of her notebook and saw the names Dr. Jonathan Mercer and Dr. Marcus Reed written across the top of the page. The name caused the detective at the table to look up, and for the first time that afternoon, a faint smile crossed his face. The coincidence had already been mentioned during the trial, but seeing it in Maria's notes made it strange all over again. Around the table, the jurors shifted from the heaviness of suffering into the steadier terrain of records and sources. No one mistook that shift for ease.

"Still strange hearing a witness with my name," Marcus said.

A few of the jurors laughed, but the humor passed quickly. The room had become too invested in the evidence to stay light for long. Maria looked around the table, then glanced back at the page where she had marked several lines from the testimony. She had taught enough history to know that the first question was not whether a source was perfect. The first question was whether the source belonged in the discussion at all.

"This part was about whether Jesus actually existed," Maria said.

Anthony Russo raised his eyebrows. "I thought everybody already agreed Jesus existed."

Rebecca Collins shifted in her seat. "I have heard people say He was invented."

Maria nodded. "People do say that. Dr. Mercer testified that serious historians usually do not take that position. The real debate is not whether Jesus existed. The debate is who He was and what happened after His death."

Leonard Shaw adjusted in his chair. He had been quieter since the discussion about suffering, though no one mistook silence for agreement. His skepticism was still there, but it no longer came as quickly or as sharply as it had earlier. Something had been exposed in him during the last discussion, and although he had not softened, he had become more careful. When he spoke, his voice carried resistance without the same edge.

"I can accept that Jesus existed," Leonard said. "That does not bother me. Lots of people existed. The problem is what Christians do with Him afterward. They take a first-century Jewish teacher and turn Him into God."

Harold Bennett looked toward Maria, giving her room to respond. He had learned not to force a religious answer into every opening. The room listened better when no one tried to rush it. Maria glanced down at her notes and found the portion of Dr. Mercer's testimony where she had written sources in the margin. That had been the strength of his testimony, at least to her. He had not begun with doctrine. He had begun with evidence.

"Dr. Mercer did not begin with theology," Maria said. "He began with sources. He talked about the Gospels, Paul's letters, and non-Christian references like Tacitus, Josephus, Pliny, and Suetonius. His point was not that every source says the same thing or that every detail is beyond question. His point was that Jesus of Nazareth belongs to history. He was not a myth created centuries later."

Patricia Nguyen had already drawn a line down the center of her page. On one side she had written Mercer. On the other, Reed. Beneath both names, she had listed areas of agreement in a careful column. Her accounting mind had kept returning to the admissions from cross-examination, and the list now seemed more important than the arguments surrounding it. She read from it without embellishment.

"I made a list of what both historians accepted," Patricia said. "Jesus existed. He was Jewish. He lived in the first century. He gained followers. He was crucified under Pontius Pilate. His followers believed He rose from the dead. Christianity spread very early. Dr. Reed questioned interpretation, but he did not deny those basic facts."

Paul Jensen leaned back, his eyes fixed on the ceiling for a moment. The testimony had affected him more than he had expected. As an atheist, he had never felt the need to study the historical Jesus closely. He had assumed the Christian story had grown out of legend, religious longing, and centuries of church tradition. He had not expected Northbridge's own historian to concede as much as he had.

"That bothered me," Paul said.

Leonard looked toward him. "What bothered you?"

Paul lowered his eyes from the ceiling and looked at the table. "I do not mean it bothered me because I think Mercer was wrong. It bothered me because I realized I had been careless. I used to say Christianity was built on mythology. I said it like I knew that. But I never actually studied the sources."

The room quieted around him. Paul looked at the notes he had taken during Dr. Reed's testimony, though he seemed to be reading more than words. "I watched videos. I read articles. I heard people say Jesus was probably borrowed from older myths or invented by the church. It felt intelligent to repeat it. Then Reed got on the stand, and even he did not say that."

Leonard frowned. "Why does that matter? A man named Jesus existed. That does not prove Christianity."

"No," Paul said. "But it removes one of my exits."

The words were plain, but they carried weight. Anthony glanced at him, and even Leonard did not immediately respond. Rebecca Collins leaned forward, curious in the way she often was when someone said something that sounded simple but opened into something larger. She had no desire to take sides too quickly. She wanted to understand what had changed in the room.

"What do you mean by exit?" Rebecca asked.

Paul rubbed his thumb along the edge of his notebook. "I mean it was easier to dismiss everything when I could tell myself the whole story was fiction. If Jesus was invented, then I did not have to take the rest seriously. But if He was real, if He was crucified, if His followers really believed something happened afterward, then I have to ask why. I do not have to accept Christianity, but I cannot dismiss it with a slogan anymore."

Anthony looked uncomfortable. "I do not like where this is going."

Paul gave a faint smile. "Neither do I."

Maria watched the exchange carefully. She had seen that look on students before, the look of someone realizing that a simple answer no longer worked. "That is what history does when you let it. It does not always give you everything you want, but it removes careless answers."

Anthony tapped his fingers against the table. "Religious documents are still biased. The Gospels were written by believers. That has to matter."

"It does matter," Maria replied. "Bias does not automatically make a source useless. Every historical source has a perspective. Roman historians had political interests. Jewish historians had religious and national interests. Government records had official agendas. Letters were written for reasons. Historians do not throw sources away because the writer cared about the subject. They ask whether the source is early, connected to the events, consistent with other evidence, and useful for reconstructing what happened."

Rebecca looked down at her notes. "I always thought if a document was religious, historians could not really use it."

"They can," Maria said. "And they do. A religious source can contain historical information. The question is whether it can be examined. Dr. Mercer never asked us to treat the Gospels like modern court transcripts. He asked us not to dismiss them simply because they were written by believers."

Leonard leaned forward. "Belief changes people. If you worship someone, you are not neutral about him."

"No historian is neutral," Maria said. "Neutrality is not the standard. Careful analysis is."

Patricia nodded. "Dr. Reed made that point too. He said the Gospels were theological documents and needed to be handled carefully, but he did not say they were worthless. He questioned how far we can go with them."

Marcus looked from Patricia to Leonard. "That is how witnesses work too. A witness can care deeply about a case and still tell the truth. A mother who watched her son get shot is not neutral. That does not mean we ignore her testimony. It means we examine it carefully, compare it with other evidence, and ask whether it holds up."

Anthony looked toward Marcus. "Witnesses can be wrong."

"Absolutely," Marcus said. "They can lie. They can remember incorrectly. They can interpret something badly. But you do not decide that before hearing them. You test them."

Sheila Morrison had been listening quietly. "And that is what Professor Price seemed to be asking for. Not blind acceptance. Examination."

Leonard looked at her sharply. "Faith always says that until you start asking the wrong questions."

Sheila did not flinch. "Then that kind of faith is weak. From what we heard, Professor Price did not punish questions. He invited them."

Leonard looked away. His expression showed that he wanted to argue, but the facts of the trial had made that harder than his anger wanted it to be. Denise Walker spoke next, and her voice brought the discussion back to the testimony without losing the human weight beneath it. She had grown up hearing about Jesus in church, but the trial had done something she had not expected. It had made familiar stories feel anchored to time and place.

"I grew up hearing about Jesus in church," Denise said. "But Mercer's testimony made me think about Him differently. I know that sounds strange. I believed in Him, but maybe I had made Him less historical in my mind without realizing it. Hearing about Judea, Rome, Pilate, crucifixion, early followers, and hostile sources made Him feel less like a figure in a stained-glass window and more like a man who stepped into real history."

Anthony gave her a guarded look. "That is exactly what worries me. People start with a real man, then build stained glass around Him."

Denise nodded. "That may be a fair concern. But it is not the same thing as saying there was no man."

Anthony did not answer. Evelyn Brooks had been quiet, turning one page of her notebook back and forth with the tips of her fingers. As a retired librarian, she had spent her life around records, biographies, old newspaper archives, damaged books, and the fragile remains of human memory. She knew how easily stories disappeared when no one cared enough to preserve them. The testimony about ancient sources had felt less abstract to her than perhaps it had to others.

"I kept thinking about how little survives from the ancient world," Evelyn said. "People today expect video, photographs, recorded interviews, and official databases. Ancient history does not work that way. We know many things from sources that are later, partial, biased, or incomplete. Dr. Mercer was right about that. The fact that Jesus appears in early Christian writings, Roman references, Jewish sources, and hostile discussions is not nothing."

Paul nodded slowly. "That is what got me. I used to hold Christianity to a standard I did not use for anything else in ancient history. If the source was Christian, I treated it as suspicious. If the source was Roman or Greek, I treated it like history. Mercer exposed that inconsistency."

Leonard's jaw tightened. "Maybe you were too careless. That does not mean the church is right."

Paul looked at him. "I know. But it means I was wrong about something."

The admission seemed to cost him something. For a man who had built much of his identity on being rational, admitting careless skepticism felt almost like confession. Maria understood that better than she let on. Students could be wrong easily when the grade was low and the stakes were small. Adults had a harder time because correction touched pride, identity, and years of conclusions built on unchecked assumptions.

Maria spoke gently. "That matters."

Paul nodded, but said nothing.

Frank Dawson had been listening without interrupting. He finally leaned forward, not as a leader forcing a conclusion, but as a man trying to keep the discussion tied to the charge they had been given. The room had a way of drifting into worldview when the evidence became personal. Frank understood why it happened, but Judge Hayes's instructions still governed them. They were not there to decide whether Paul should believe. They were there to decide whether Professor Price had been punished unlawfully.

"Let's bring this back to Professor Price," Frank said. "Northbridge accused him of presenting religious conclusions as though they could be discussed as truth. If his claim was that Jesus actually existed, Mercer and Reed both support the idea that this is a legitimate historical discussion. The disagreement begins after that."

Patricia glanced at her two-column list again. "Exactly. If Professor Price said Jesus existed, he was on solid historical ground. If he said Jesus was crucified under Pontius Pilate, that was also supported. If he said the followers of Jesus believed He rose, even Reed accepted that. The dispute is interpretation."

Leonard raised a finger slightly. "And interpretation is where religion enters."

Maria nodded. "Yes. But interpretation is part of history. Historians interpret evidence all the time."

Leonard shook his head. "Not like this. Not when the interpretation is that the man was God."

Harold leaned forward. "We are not there yet. This part of the testimony was only about whether Jesus existed and whether the early movement was grounded in real events. We need to take the evidence in order."

Anthony looked toward Leonard. "I hate to say it, but he is right. We cannot jump ahead."

Leonard looked irritated by Anthony's agreement with Harold. "Now you too?"

Anthony shrugged. "I still do not trust religious people with power. I still think churches can twist stories to control people. But if we are talking about whether Jesus existed, I do not think Northbridge denied it."

Rebecca Collins scanned her notes. "They did not. Dr. Reed kept saying the issue was not existence, but development of tradition and theological interpretation."

Maria pointed toward Rebecca. "That is right."

Paul let out a slow breath. "Which means the skeptical position was not that Jesus was made up. It was that the story grew around Him."

"Yes," Maria said.

"And that is a different argument," Paul said.

"It is."

Paul sat back, troubled by the distinction. He had spent years thinking of faith as an escape from evidence. Now he was beginning to feel that some of his unbelief had been an escape of its own. Marcus watched him with the trained eye of a detective, not prying, but noticing. The change in Paul was not conversion. It was something more uncomfortable for him than that. It was the loss of an easy dismissal.

"You all right?" Marcus asked.

Paul smiled faintly. "I do not know. I think I preferred being certain."

Leonard gave a dry laugh. "Welcome to the club."

The room relaxed for a moment, but only slightly. Beneath the humor, something serious was happening. The atheists in the room were not becoming believers, not yet, and perhaps not ever. The easy dismissals were beginning to fail. Jesus could no longer be treated as a myth without evidence. The Gospels could no longer be dismissed simply because believers wrote them. The early Christian movement could no longer be explained away as a vague legend from centuries later. The facts did not force a verdict of faith, but they demanded more respect than some of the jurors had been prepared to give.

Denise looked toward Paul. "Does that scare you?"

Paul thought about the question. He could have brushed it aside, but the room had become too honest for that. "A little. Not because I am afraid of church. I am not. Not because I am afraid of Christians. No offense, but most of them do not scare me."

Harold smiled faintly. "None taken."

Paul continued. "It scares me because I thought I had already examined this and rejected it. Now I am realizing I may have rejected a version of it I never really examined."

That struck harder than he intended. Anthony looked down. Rebecca stopped writing. Leonard turned toward the narrow window in the door, his expression unreadable. Sheila's voice was quiet when she spoke.

"That is not a small realization."

"No," Paul said. "It is not."

Maria looked back at the page where she had written Mercer's main conclusion. Jesus of Nazareth was not merely a subject of faith. He was a figure of history. She remembered the way Rebecca Kane had tried to separate belief from fact during cross-examination, and how Mercer had refused to let the categories remain clean. Christianity made claims about public events. If those claims were false, they could be challenged. If they were true, they could not be dismissed merely because they were religious.

Frank finally reached for his pen. He had promised himself he would not reduce every discussion to a phrase, but the habit was difficult to resist. This time he did not place the legal pad in the center of the table or make a performance of writing. He simply noted the point in his own space.

Jesus historical; meaning disputed.

Leonard noticed but said nothing.

The silence that followed was not empty. Each juror seemed to be measuring the same conclusion from a different angle. For Harold and Sheila, the historical testimony strengthened what they already believed. For Maria and Evelyn, it confirmed that faith and history were not enemies. For Anthony, it created discomfort because the line between religious abuse and historical truth was becoming harder to manage. For Leonard, it threatened one of the walls he had built between his father's hypocrisy and the possibility that God might still be real. For Paul, it did something even more dangerous. It made unbelief feel less like certainty and more like a position that also had to be defended.

Frank looked around the table. "So where does that leave us?"

Maria answered first. "It leaves us with a real man in real history."

Patricia added, "And with agreement between both historians on the core facts."

Marcus nodded. "And with disagreement over interpretation, not existence."

Anthony rubbed his face, then lowered his hands to the table. "I can accept that. I do not like what Christians do with it, but I can accept that."

Leonard spoke without looking up. "I can accept Jesus existed. I can accept He was crucified. I can accept His followers believed something. That still does not make Him God."

Harold did not argue. "No. But it means the next question matters."

Rebecca looked at him. "What next question?"

Harold turned slightly toward Maria's notes, where the next section waited. "If He existed, then we have to ask who He claimed to be."

No one rushed to respond. The room had followed the evidence from the universe to life, from morality to suffering, and now to a man from Nazareth whose existence even the skeptical witnesses had not denied. The question no longer felt distant. It was becoming narrower, more personal, and harder to avoid.

Paul closed his notebook, then opened it again. "That is the question I was hoping we would not get to."

Anthony looked at him. "Why?"

Paul stared at the witness list. "Because if Jesus was just a myth, none of this matters. If He was only a misunderstood teacher, then Christianity is exaggerated. But if He actually claimed what Christians say He claimed, then dismissing Him gets a lot harder."

Leonard stood and walked to the window, not because he had anywhere to go, but because sitting had become uncomfortable. "You people are getting ahead of yourselves."

"Maybe," Paul said. "But not by much."

The room remained quiet as Leonard looked out through the narrow pane of glass in the door. Beyond it, the courthouse hallway was empty. Inside the deliberation room, the twelve jurors sat with the weight of a historical question that had become more than historical. Jesus had existed. That did not settle who He was. It meant the next question could not be ignored.

# 19

THE QUESTION DID NOT leave the room after Harold asked it. If Jesus existed, then they had to ask who He claimed to be. For several minutes, no one opened another notebook or reached for another cup of coffee. The jurors had followed the evidence this far almost against their own instincts, moving from the universe to life, from morality to suffering, and from suffering into history. Now the discussion narrowed around one man, one life, and one claim that could not be treated as harmless if it was true.

Maria Alvarez finally turned the page. She did it slowly, as if the movement itself required a decision. The next names were Dr. Richard Callahan and Rabbi Daniel Cohen. She remembered their testimony well because it had not sounded like a simple argument between a Christian and a skeptic. Rabbi Cohen had not been hostile. He had been thoughtful, devout, and deeply respectful of the Jewish Scriptures. He had rejected the Christian interpretation of Jesus, but he had not dismissed the question as foolish, and that made the testimony more difficult rather than less.

"The next witnesses were Dr. Richard Callahan and Rabbi Daniel Cohen," Maria said. "This was about what Jesus claimed about Himself."

Leonard turned from the window and came back to the table. His face had hardened again, but the hardness no longer looked as secure as it had earlier. "This is where Christians make the jump. Jesus existed, fine. He taught. He gathered followers. He got killed. Then people start saying He claimed to be God, and that is where I do not follow."

Harold watched him without answering. He knew this part of the discussion could not be forced. If he pushed too quickly, Leonard would retreat behind anger. If he said too little, the room would drift back into easy categories. Maria looked down at her notes, giving the answer from the testimony rather than from her own beliefs.

"Dr. Callahan's argument was that Jesus made claims that would have been understood as divine in His Jewish context," Maria said. "He talked about Jesus forgiving sins, calling Himself the Son of Man from Daniel, saying before Abraham was, I am, and being accused of blasphemy. His point was that Jesus was not merely offering general moral teaching."

Anthony Russo leaned forward, his expression sharp. "But Rabbi Cohen disagreed. That is important. He said Jews do not accept that interpretation. He said Christians read later theology back into the text."

"He did," Maria said. "And I thought he was one of the strongest witnesses Northbridge called."

Sheila nodded. "So did I."

Anthony looked surprised. "You did?"

"Yes," Sheila said. "He was serious. He was careful. He knew the Scriptures. He did not reject Christianity because he had never thought about it. He rejected it because he believed the Christian conclusion was wrong."

Leonard pointed toward Sheila as if she had finally said something he could use. "Exactly. So why are we acting like Callahan settled anything?"

Paul Jensen had been quiet since the last round of discussion. His notes were open in front of him, but he was no longer reading them. He was staring at the witness names as if they had turned into something personal.

"I do not think Callahan settled it," Paul said. "But Cohen did not erase it either."

Leonard looked at him with visible frustration. "You keep doing that."

"Doing what?"

"Moving the goalpost," Leonard said. "First it was whether Jesus existed. Now He existed, so it is whether He claimed too much. If we get past that, then it will be whether He rose. This thing never ends."

Paul looked up at him. "Maybe that is because the evidence keeps going."

Leonard's chair scraped against the floor as he sat back. "Or maybe it is because religion always finds another way to keep itself alive."

The words landed hard. Anthony nodded as if he understood the instinct behind them, but Denise looked uncomfortable. Harold's jaw tightened, though he said nothing. The room had become warm, and the stale air seemed to make every word heavier. Marcus Reed, the detective, looked toward Leonard with the patience of someone used to separating anger from evidence.

"Leonard, that is not an answer to the testimony."

Leonard turned on him. "And what is the answer? That Jesus was God because Christians say He was?"

"No," Marcus said evenly. "The question is whether Callahan gave evidence that Jesus made extraordinary claims. I do not have to be a theologian to see that the trial gave us something to examine. Jesus forgiving sins is not a small thing in that context. The blasphemy charge is not a small thing. The reaction of His opponents matters."

Anthony shook his head. "People get accused of things they do not mean all the time."

"True," Marcus said. "But repeated reactions matter. Patterns matter."

Patricia Nguyen tapped the page where she had outlined Callahan's testimony. "What struck me was that Callahan did not rely on one statement. He built a cumulative argument. Forgiving sins. Lord of the Sabbath. Son of Man. I am. One with the Father. The trial before the high priest. Each one can be debated, but together they form a pattern."

Leonard leaned toward her. "Or Christians arranged the pattern later."

Patricia did not flinch. "That is exactly what Rabbi Cohen argued may have happened in places. But he still admitted Jesus' followers worshiped Him very early. He admitted the earliest Christians, many of them Jewish, came to believe things about Jesus that would have been shocking inside Judaism."

Maria added, "And that is historically significant. A group of first-century Jews did not easily begin worshiping a man. Something had to explain that."

Leonard laughed, but there was no humor in it. "Something had to explain it, so God?"

Paul's voice sharpened before anyone expected it. "Stop doing that."

The room froze.

Leonard stared at him. "What did you say?"

Paul sat forward, his face flushed now, the controlled, analytical calm that had defined him since deliberations began finally breaking. "I said stop doing that. Every time someone raises a point you do not like, you reduce it to a slogan. Nobody said, something happened, therefore God. Maria said there is a historical problem. Patricia said there is a pattern. Marcus said the accusations matter. You do not have to agree, but you are not answering them. You are making the argument sound stupid so you do not have to deal with it."

Leonard's eyes narrowed. "And you believe it now? Is that what this is?"

"No," Paul said, though his voice had lost some certainty. "I do not know what I believe. That is the problem. I came in here thinking I knew exactly what Christianity was. I thought it was comfort for people who could not handle reality. I thought the Bible was a pile of legends. I thought Jesus was probably a preacher who got exaggerated into a god. The more we go through this, the more I realize I dismissed things I never actually examined."

Anthony looked between them. "Paul, you do not have to defend Christianity to be fair."

"I am not defending Christianity," Paul said. "I am defending the evidence from lazy answers. Some of my answers were lazy."

That silenced the room more than his anger had. Leonard looked away first. Rebecca Collins spoke carefully, almost reluctantly, as though she knew her question would pull the room deeper into the same place Paul had just entered.

"I do not know all the theology," Rebecca said. "But I remember when Callahan explained the Son of Man title. I always thought that meant Jesus was emphasizing His humanity. Callahan said in Daniel it was connected to authority, dominion, and a kingdom that would not pass away. That surprised me."

Maria nodded. "That was one of his strongest points."

Rebecca continued, gaining confidence. "Then Rabbi Cohen said Christians misunderstand it, or at least take it further than Judaism allows. I understood that. But it still seemed like Jesus was saying something bigger than just, be nice to people."

Sheila looked at Rebecca with a gentle expression. "That is the question. Was Jesus simply a moral teacher, or did He place Himself at the center of God's authority?"

Anthony rubbed both hands over his face. "I hate this part."

Denise looked at him. "Why?"

"Because I like Jesus," Anthony said. "I know that sounds strange. I do not trust church. I do not trust priests. I do not trust religious systems. But Jesus, at least the parts I remember, seems different. He cared about the poor. He touched lepers. He forgave people nobody else wanted. He went after hypocrites. I can respect that Jesus."

Harold leaned forward. "But?"

Anthony looked at him. "But when people start saying He is God, that is when religion gets power. That is when people start speaking for Him. That is when men in robes and pulpits tell everyone else what God wants."

Sheila answered softly. "Maybe. But if Jesus truly claimed divine authority, then the problem is not that people took Him too seriously. The problem is that some used His name while refusing to live like Him."

Anthony's face tightened. "That is too easy."

"No," Sheila said. "It is not easy at all. It means people like the man who hurt your brother did not merely fail a church. They sinned against the Christ they claimed to represent."

Anthony looked down at the table, his jaw working as if he had a response but could not bring it out without saying too much. Harold spoke next, not to win the argument, but to name what everyone felt.

"That is why the identity of Jesus matters," Harold said. "If He was only a teacher, then people can admire Him, quote Him, and move on. But if He is who He claimed to be, then none of us can use Him. We answer to Him."

The room stayed quiet. Leonard finally spoke, his voice lower than before. "You people keep saying claimed to be. How do we know He actually said those things? How do we know His followers did not put words in His mouth after He died?"

Maria glanced down at her notes from Rabbi Cohen. "That was Rabbi Cohen's strongest challenge. He questioned whether the later Gospel language reflected the developed faith of the Christian community."

"Exactly," Leonard said.

"But Callahan answered with more than John," Maria continued. "He used Mark too. He used the forgiveness of sins. He used the Son of Man language. He used the trial scene. He argued that even the earlier material shows Jesus acting and speaking with unusual authority."

Patricia added, "And Cohen did not deny that Jesus was perceived as making dangerous claims. He rejected the Christian conclusion, but he did not reduce Jesus to a harmless moralist."

Marcus nodded. "That matters. People do not usually crucify harmless moralists."

Leonard's voice rose. "Rome crucified troublemakers. That is what Rome did."

"Yes," Marcus said. "But the Jewish leadership's charge had religious weight. Blasphemy. Authority. Claims about God's place. Callahan was not making that up."

Paul picked up his notes and read from the line he had underlined during the trial. "Callahan said, 'Jesus did not merely point people to God. He spoke as though the response to Him was the response to God.'"

Leonard stood again, anger flashing. "Do you hear yourself? You are quoting the Christian witness like it is Scripture now."

Paul stood halfway out of his chair, then stopped himself. "I am quoting testimony."

"You are changing," Leonard said.

Paul's face went still. "Maybe I am."

The honesty of it took the room by surprise. Paul sat back down, but he did not look away.

"I do not know whether I believe Jesus is God," Paul said. "Saying that out loud still sounds impossible to me. But I know this. I can no longer call it ridiculous without lying. That bothers me more than anything that has happened in this room."

Rebecca Collins looked at him with wide eyes. "Why does it bother you?"

Paul swallowed. "Because if Jesus claimed to be God, then He is not just an idea I can reject from a distance. He becomes someone I have to deal with."

Anthony whispered almost to himself, "That is what scares people."

No one asked him to explain. Evelyn Brooks had been watching Leonard since Paul spoke. Her voice was quiet when she entered the discussion.

"Leonard, may I ask you something?"

Leonard looked at her warily. "You can ask."

"Would you be angry if Jesus were real, or only if the religion around Him were real?"

The question unsettled him. He opened his mouth, then closed it. For a moment, the man who had argued with nearly everyone in the room seemed unable to find the familiar path back to defiance.

"I do not know," he said finally.

Evelyn nodded as if that answer mattered. "I think I understand that. After my husband died, I thought I was angry at God. Later, I wondered if I was angry at the things people said about God. Sometimes those are not the same."

Leonard sat slowly. "My father made them the same."

The room seemed to bend around the sentence. Harold looked at him with compassion, though he chose his words carefully.

"Then your father lied about God with his life."

Leonard's face flushed. "You do not know that."

"No," Harold said. "I do not know him. But I know this. If Jesus is anything like what the Gospels show, then your father did not represent Him when he terrorized your home. He betrayed Him."

Leonard's eyes glistened, though he blinked quickly and looked away before anyone could linger on it. Anthony stared at the table, and for the first time, his anger and Leonard's seemed to recognize each other without needing words. Denise spoke with the tenderness of someone accustomed to pain.

"Maybe that is why this question hurts so much," Denise said. "If Jesus was only a teacher, then people can use Him and ruin Him for others. If He is Lord, then the people who used His name to harm others do not get the final word on who He is."

Sheila nodded, her eyes damp. "Exactly."

Leonard wiped at his face with the heel of his hand, angry at himself for showing anything. "I do not want a sermon."

Denise's voice remained soft. "I was not giving one."

Frank, sensing the room nearing a breaking point, brought them carefully back to the evidence. He did not want to flatten what had just happened, but he also knew they needed a place to stand. The legal issue had not disappeared simply because the testimony had reached into wounds. If anything, the wounds made discipline more necessary.

"We need to stay with Callahan and Cohen," Frank said. "What can we agree on from their testimony?"

Maria took a breath. "We can agree that Jesus was not presented by either side as a harmless figure."

Patricia nodded. "We can agree that His followers understood Him in divine terms very early."

Marcus added, "We can agree there is serious debate about whether Jesus Himself made those claims or whether the church developed them, but Callahan gave evidence that the claims go back into the earliest traditions."

Sheila said, "And Rabbi Cohen, while rejecting the Christian conclusion, did not treat the issue as foolish."

Anthony spoke slowly, as though each word required more effort than usual. "I can agree with that. Cohen did not sound like a man dismissing nonsense. He sounded like a man rejecting something he understood."

Harold looked at him. "That is a fair distinction."

Paul stared at the witness list again. "I can agree that Jesus cannot be reduced to a nice teacher without ignoring a lot of evidence."

Leonard looked at him but did not argue this time.

Rebecca asked, "Is that why Professor Price said Jesus forces a decision?"

Maria turned toward her. "Yes. That was his claim. If Jesus truly made divine claims, then people cannot simply place Him among moral teachers and walk away."

Leonard spoke under his breath, but everyone heard him. "Maybe I wanted to walk away."

The room was still. Paul looked at him differently now, not as an opponent, but as a man standing in a different place on the same road.

"Me too," Paul said.

For the first time all day, Leonard did not push back. He looked exhausted, as if the argument itself had cost him more than he had intended to pay. Frank wrote a small note in the margin of his own paper, not in the center of the table this time and not for effect. He wrote it because he needed to remember where the discussion had landed.

Jesus' claims serious; rejection not simple.

When he looked up, the others were quiet. Harold was looking down at the table. Anthony sat rigidly, fighting memories that had nothing to do with the courtroom and everything to do with what men had done in the name of God. Paul looked shaken, not converted, but no longer untouched. Leonard looked angry, wounded, and afraid of what might happen if the walls he had built began to crack.

The question had changed shape in the room. It was no longer merely whether Professor Price had the right to teach that Jesus claimed divine authority. That mattered legally, and they would return to it. Beneath the legal question, something else had begun to stir. If Jesus had claimed what Callahan said He claimed, then the jurors were not only evaluating Professor Price. They were being forced to evaluate their own distance from the man at the center of the trial.

No verdict had been reached. No one had changed sides completely. Something had shifted, and everyone knew it. By the time Frank suggested they stop for a short break, no one objected. They needed air, silence, and a few minutes away from the table where the question of Jesus had become more personal than any of them expected.

As they stood, Paul remained seated, staring at the words he had written in his notebook during Callahan's testimony. Not merely teacher. He closed the notebook slowly, but the words stayed with him.

# 20

When the jurors came back from the break, no one seemed eager to sit down. Anthony lingered near the counter where the coffee had gone cold. Leonard stood by the narrow window in the door, looking out into the hallway as though an answer might be waiting somewhere beyond the glass. Paul returned to his chair but did not open his notebook right away. He had spent the break alone, staring at the courthouse wall and trying to decide whether the uneasiness inside him was intellectual honesty or the beginning of something he did not want.

Maria waited until everyone had settled before turning to the next section of her notes. She already knew where the discussion was headed. The trial had moved toward this point from the beginning, even when the testimony seemed to be about other things. The universe, life, morality, suffering, history, and the claims of Jesus had all narrowed into one question. Christianity did not rest merely on the idea that Jesus was wise, kind, misunderstood, or unjustly executed. It rested on whether something happened after His death.

"The next witnesses were Dr. William Grant and Dr. Richard Ellis," Maria said. "The resurrection."

Rebecca Collins looked from Maria to the others, her pen resting against the edge of her notebook. "Can I ask something before we argue about whether it happened?"

Maria nodded. "Of course."

Rebecca hesitated, as if she were afraid the question might sound foolish. "Has anyone asked why it matters so much? I understand that Christians believe Jesus rose from the dead, and I understand that it would be a miracle. But why is that the center of everything? Why is His teaching not enough? Why is His death not enough? What is so important about Him rising from the dead?"

The question quieted the room in a different way. It was not hostile and it was not sarcastic. It was the question of someone who had listened carefully and realized that the entire trial had been moving toward a claim she still did not fully understand. Sheila Morrison looked at Rebecca with a tenderness that did not feel forced. She answered as one teacher speaking to another student of the question.

"Because if Jesus only taught good things and then died, He would be remembered as a teacher," Sheila said. "Maybe even a prophet. But if He rose from the dead, then God confirmed who He was. The resurrection would mean His claims were not just words. It would mean death did not defeat Him."

Harold leaned forward. "It also means Christianity is not built merely on moral advice. It is built on an event. If Jesus did not rise, then the Christian faith collapses. But if He did rise, then everything He said about God, sin, forgiveness, judgment, and eternal life has to be taken seriously."

Paul stared at the page in front of him. The answer bothered him because it was exactly what he had been trying not to admit. "So the resurrection is not just a miracle added to the story," he said. "It is the verdict on Jesus Himself."

Sheila nodded. "Yes. That is why it matters."

Anthony shifted in his chair, visibly uncomfortable. "So if He stayed dead, He is just another religious teacher."

Harold answered carefully. "If He stayed dead, then Christianity becomes memory, morality, and tradition. But if He rose, then He is not merely someone people remember. He is someone people must answer to."

Rebecca looked down and wrote something in her notebook. "That makes the question feel a lot bigger."

Paul looked at her, then at the witness list. "It is bigger," he said quietly. "That is the problem."

Leonard turned from the window with open resistance in his face. "Dead people do not rise."

He did not shout, but his voice had enough force to pull every eye toward him. Harold did not answer immediately. He had learned that some statements were not merely arguments. They were walls. Leonard had just placed one in the center of the room.

"No one is saying dead people usually rise," Harold said. "That is the whole reason the claim matters."

Leonard walked back to his chair but did not sit. "No, that is the reason the claim fails. We do not need three weeks of testimony to know dead is dead."

Paul finally opened his notebook. His hand rested on the page where he had written Grant's name, Ellis's name, and a list of facts both men had discussed. "I used to say the same thing," Paul said. "I still want to say it."

Leonard looked at him. "Then say it."

Paul looked down at his notes. "I cannot say it the same way anymore."

Anthony leaned forward, suddenly alert. "What does that mean?"

Paul took a breath. "It means I used to reject the resurrection because miracles are impossible. But I only believed miracles were impossible because I believed God did not exist. After everything we have gone through, I am not as certain of that as I was. So now I cannot just say, dead people do not rise, and pretend that settles it. If God exists, then the question changes."

Leonard stared at him as if Paul had betrayed something unspoken between them. "You hear yourself, right?"

"Yes," Paul said. "That is why I am uncomfortable."

Patricia Nguyen looked between them before bringing the discussion back to the testimony. She had outlined Grant and Ellis carefully, hoping facts would hold steady where emotions could not. "Dr. Grant did not begin by asking us to believe a miracle. He began with historical facts that he said many scholars accept: Jesus died by crucifixion, His followers believed they saw Him alive afterward, the resurrection message began very early, Paul converted, James converted, and the movement spread in Jerusalem. He also argued for the empty tomb, though Ellis was more cautious about that."

Maria nodded. "And Dr. Ellis did not deny everything. He rejected the resurrection as the best explanation, but he accepted several of the underlying facts."

Leonard sat down heavily. "Underlying facts do not raise a corpse."

Marcus Reed looked across the table. "No, but they create a case that has to be explained."

Leonard turned toward him. "You are a detective. If somebody came into your office and said a dead man walked out of a grave, would you believe him?"

Marcus did not take offense. He had expected the question. "No. Not immediately. I would test the claim. I would ask whether the person was really dead. I would ask who saw him afterward. I would ask whether the body was missing. I would ask whether witnesses had motive to lie. I would look for alternative explanations. That is exactly what Grant and Ellis were arguing about."

Anthony pointed toward Marcus. "But at the end of the day, you would look for the natural explanation first."

"Always," Marcus said. "But if every natural explanation failed to account for the evidence, I would have a problem."

The room grew tighter. The resurrection testimony had not felt like the earlier discussions. With the universe, the jurors could remain observers. With morality, they had become participants. With suffering, they had become wounded people sitting around a table. The resurrection demanded a verdict in a way the other questions had not. If Jesus remained dead, Christianity could still be admired as an ethical system or studied as a historical movement. If He rose, admiration was no longer enough.

Denise Walker looked down at the notes she had taken during Dr. Grant's testimony. "I remember when Grant said Christianity could have died in Jerusalem if the body had been produced. That stayed with me. The message began in the same city where Jesus was crucified. That seems important."

Leonard shook his head. "Or the body was moved. Or stolen. Or lost. Or the story developed later."

Maria answered carefully. "Grant addressed those. He argued that the stolen body theory does not explain why the disciples would suffer for something they knew was false. He argued that legend does not explain how early the resurrection message appeared. He mentioned the creed in First Corinthians as very early."

Anthony looked uneasy. "People suffer for false things all the time."

"Yes," Sheila said. "But Grant's point was that people may die for something false if they believe it is true. They do not usually die for something they know they invented."

Anthony looked at her sharply. "Usually is doing a lot of work there."

Sheila accepted the criticism with a small nod. "It is. History rarely gives mathematical certainty. It does allow us to weigh explanations."

Paul ran his hand through his hair. "The hallucination theory bothered me too."

Leonard almost laughed. "You mean it did not help?"

"It helped until Stone started asking questions," Paul said. "Hallucinations might explain one person seeing something. Maybe a few. But Grant argued that hallucinations do not explain group appearances, the empty tomb, James, Paul, and the rise of the movement in Jerusalem. Ellis admitted no single natural explanation accounts for everything."

Patricia checked her notes. "He said he preferred several natural explanations together rather than one miracle."

"That sounds reasonable," Anthony said.

"It does," Paul replied. "But it also feels like stacking possibilities to avoid one conclusion."

Leonard's face hardened. "Because the one conclusion is impossible."

Paul leaned toward him. "That is the question, Leonard. Is it impossible, or do you need it to be impossible?"

The room went quiet.

Leonard's eyes flashed. "Careful."

Paul did not back away this time. "No. I am asking because I have to ask myself the same thing. I needed it to be impossible because if it was impossible, I did not have to deal with Jesus. If miracles cannot happen, then the resurrection is off the table before the evidence is even presented. That was easy. Now I am wondering if easy is what I was protecting."

Anthony looked at Paul with a mixture of worry and irritation. "You sound like you are halfway across the river."

Paul gave a strained smile. "I do not even know where the river is."

Rebecca Collins had been listening with her notebook open, but she had stopped writing. Her face carried the confusion of someone who had not come into the room with a hardened position and therefore felt every argument more directly. "I do not understand something," she said. "Dr. Ellis said historians cannot prove miracles because history deals with normal events. But if something unusual happened, would history still have to deal with the evidence it left behind?"

Maria looked pleased by the question. "That is exactly the issue. Historians cannot recreate the resurrection in a laboratory. They cannot observe it directly. But they can examine the aftermath. They can ask what best explains the facts."

Rebecca looked at Leonard. "So saying miracles do not happen before looking at the evidence is not really history. It is a rule you bring with you."

Leonard stared at her for a long moment. "You too?"

Rebecca flushed slightly but did not retreat. "I am not saying I believe it happened. I am saying I understand Paul's point. If God does not exist, then resurrection is impossible. But if God might exist, then maybe the evidence has to be weighed differently."

Harold looked at Paul, then Rebecca, but said nothing. He did not want to ruin the moment by claiming it for his side. Evelyn Brooks placed both hands near her notebook. Her voice was quiet, but the room had learned to listen when she spoke.

"When Dr. Grant talked about the disciples, I kept thinking about grief," Evelyn said. "People in grief can imagine things. They can hear voices, see faces, feel someone's presence. I know that. After my husband died, I thought I saw him in a grocery store once. For one second, I was certain. Then the man turned around, and it was not him."

Denise looked at her gently.

Evelyn continued. "So I understand why Ellis suggested visions or grief experiences. That explanation made sense to me at first. But grief did not make me believe my husband had conquered death. It did not make me go into the street and announce that history had changed. It did not make his brother, who had doubted him, suddenly worship him. It did not turn an enemy into a missionary."

Paul looked up when she mentioned an enemy. He had written Saul of Tarsus in the margin of his notes. "Paul's conversion is a problem."

Anthony frowned. "People change religions."

"Yes," Paul said. "But Saul was not looking for Christianity. He was trying to destroy it. Grant made that point. Something happened that he believed was an encounter with the risen Jesus. Ellis said it could have been visionary, psychological, maybe guilt. But that does not explain why it happened to someone so hostile, or why he was willing to suffer afterward."

Leonard gripped his coffee cup. "People are complicated."

"That is not an explanation," Paul said.

"It is more honest than pretending we know what happened two thousand years ago."

Maria intervened before the tension broke into open hostility. "We do not know with modern certainty. Ancient history never gives that kind of certainty. The question is which explanation accounts for the most facts with the fewest problems."

Marcus nodded. "That is how cases work too. You do not get certainty about every second. You get evidence, witnesses, motives, contradictions, and probabilities."

Leonard looked at him. "And if the defendant says a miracle happened?"

Marcus leaned back. "Then I would need extraordinary evidence."

"Exactly."

Marcus held his gaze. "But I would still examine the evidence."

The answer did not satisfy Leonard, but it stopped him for the moment. Anthony stood and paced toward the counter, then turned back to the group. His discomfort had been growing with every question, and the resurrection made it harder for him to keep the discussion at a safe distance.

"I do not like this," Anthony said. "I really do not. I can handle a historical Jesus. I can even handle that He made big claims. Resurrection is different. If He rose, then everything changes. That is not just an idea. That is not just church talk. That means God stepped into the world and put His hand on one man."

Sheila's voice was soft. "Yes."

Anthony looked at her. "Do not say it like it is easy."

"It is not easy," she said. "It is enormous."

He stared at her, then looked away. "My brother prayed for years after what happened to him. He used to ask God to take the memories away. They did not go away. So when people tell me God raises the dead, I wonder why He could not heal a living man."

Denise's eyes filled with sadness. "Anthony, I do not know why."

Anthony gave a bitter laugh. "At least you are honest."

"I have to be," Denise said. "I have watched too many people suffer to pretend answers are simple."

Harold looked at Anthony with compassion. "The resurrection does not mean every wound is healed immediately. It means death and evil do not get the final word."

Anthony's expression tightened. "That sounds like something people say when they cannot fix anything."

"Sometimes it is," Harold admitted. "But if Jesus rose, it is more than a saying. It is a promise grounded in an event."

Anthony sat back down slowly, as if the weight of that possibility made standing difficult. Leonard's anger returned, but there was fear beneath it now.

"And what about the people who do not get their miracle?" Leonard asked. "What about the people buried and forgotten? What about my mother? What about every prayer that hit the ceiling and died there?"

The words came faster than he intended. His face darkened as soon as he said them, as if he had revealed too much again. Paul answered before Harold could.

"That is why I do not want this to be true."

Leonard stared at him. "What?"

Paul's voice was quieter now. "If Jesus rose, then God is real in a way I cannot control. That does not make suffering easier. It might make it harder at first. Because then I have to ask why He acts sometimes and not others. Why that tomb and not every grave. Why that miracle and not every hospital room. I do not want those questions."

Denise nodded slowly. "But if He did not rise, what do we have?"

Paul looked down at his hands. "Memories. Biology. Silence. Maybe courage if we can manufacture it. Maybe justice if people manage to deliver it before they die."

No one spoke.

Paul continued. "That used to be enough for me because I called it honesty. Now I am not sure if it was honesty or resignation."

The room felt smaller. The resurrection was no longer only an ancient claim. It had reached into Leonard's childhood home, Anthony's wounded brother, Evelyn's empty house, Denise's hospital rooms, and Paul's carefully constructed unbelief. It had become the line between a universe where death was final and a universe where death had been challenged.

Patricia cleared her throat, not to diminish the emotion in the room, but to gather it into order. "What did Ellis ultimately admit?"

Maria checked her notes. "He admitted Jesus died by crucifixion. He admitted the disciples believed they saw Him alive. He admitted Paul's conversion was significant. He admitted Christianity began early. He admitted that if God exists, resurrection is possible. But he said historians should prefer natural explanations."

Frank, who had stayed quiet longer than usual, finally spoke. "That is a fair position."

Harold nodded. "It is."

Frank looked around the room. "But Grant's position was also fair. He argued that the resurrection best explains the evidence. Whether we agree with him or not, I do not see how we can call the argument reckless."

Leonard said nothing.

Maria looked toward him. "Leonard?"

He kept his eyes on the table. "I hate this one."

No one pressed him.

"I hate it because I cannot dismiss it as easily as I want to," Leonard said. "I still think dead people stay dead. I still think there has to be another explanation. But Ellis did not give one explanation. He gave possibilities. Grant gave an argument. I do not like admitting that, but it is true."

Paul's shoulders lowered slightly, as if he had been holding his breath for several minutes. Anthony looked at Leonard, then at Paul.

"So where does that leave us?" Anthony asked.

Marcus answered like a detective summarizing a case that had not yet gone to verdict. "It leaves us with facts both sides accepted and competing explanations. One explanation says something extraordinary happened. The other says several ordinary things may have combined in ways we cannot fully reconstruct. The question is not which one makes us comfortable. The question is which one Professor Price had the right to present as reasonable."

Rebecca looked down at her notebook. "And did he?"

No one answered immediately.

Sheila finally spoke. "Yes."

Harold nodded. "Yes."

Maria looked at her notes, then at the faces around the table. "I think he did."

Patricia said, "I do not know if I believe the resurrection, but I believe the argument was serious."

Denise whispered, "So do I."

Anthony hesitated. "I do not know what I believe. But I cannot say he had no evidence."

Marcus agreed. "Neither can I."

Evelyn looked toward Paul.

Paul did not answer right away. He turned back to the page where he had written, if God exists, resurrection possible. Beneath it, during Grant's testimony, he had written another sentence he had not wanted anyone to see. He closed his notebook before anyone could read it.

"I think Price had the right to say the resurrection is the best explanation," Paul said. "I do not know if he is right. But I cannot honestly say it is blind faith anymore."

Everyone turned to Leonard.

He looked at them one by one, irritated by the attention and shaken by what had happened in the room. His defenses had not collapsed, but they had cracked enough for him to feel the cold air coming through.

"I still do not believe it," he said.

Frank waited.

Leonard swallowed. "But I cannot call it nonsense."

The room did not celebrate. No one smiled. No one treated the admission as victory. It was too costly for that. Frank reached for his pen, then stopped. This time he did not write anything. The words did not need to be captured. Everyone had heard them.

For the first time since deliberations began, the resurrection had not been dismissed as impossible before being considered. It had been argued, resisted, questioned, and weighed. It had unsettled the atheists, strengthened the believers, disturbed the wounded, and forced the undecided to look more closely at what they had assumed. The verdict was not finished, but something in the room had changed.

Paul opened his notebook again and stared at the last line he had written. He did not show it to anyone. He did not say it aloud. The sentence frightened him because it no longer felt like an abstract question.

If He rose, what does that require of me?

# 21

Paul Jensen closed his notebook, but the question he had written inside would not close with it. If He rose, what does that require of me? He had not meant to write it. He had not meant to let the thought take shape at all. Questions were safer when they remained academic, when they could be handled like theories, weighed like probabilities, and stored in the mind without touching the heart. This question refused to stay there.

The room had changed. No one announced it, but everyone felt it. Earlier in the day, they had been jurors discussing expert testimony. Now they were twelve people sitting around a table with their own wounds, fears, memories, and defenses exposed. The evidence had done more than challenge Northbridge's dismissal of Professor Price. It had reached into private places each of them had tried to protect.

Anthony Russo rubbed his hands together and stared at the floor. He had stopped pacing. Leonard Shaw sat near the window, his face turned away from the others. Evelyn Brooks held a tissue in one hand but did not use it. Rebecca Collins had written almost nothing since the resurrection discussion began. Maria Alvarez watched them all with the practiced concern of a teacher who knew when a classroom had stopped being about the lesson and started being about the students.

Frank Dawson cleared his throat, though even he did not sound ready to move on. "We have gone through the major witnesses," he said. "The universe, life, morality, suffering, history, the claims of Jesus, and the resurrection. Before we talk about a verdict, I think we need to be honest about where everyone is."

Leonard turned from the window. "We are not here to share feelings."

Frank did not react sharply. "No. We are here to deliberate honestly. Honesty includes admitting when the evidence has affected us."

Leonard looked around the table with open suspicion. "So that is what this is now? A revival meeting?"

Sheila Morrison's expression tightened, but she kept her voice calm. "No. No one is asking for that."

"Feels like it."

Paul looked up. "It feels like that because some of us are changing."

The room went still.

Leonard stared at him. "Say that again."

Paul swallowed, realizing he had crossed a line he had not intended to cross publicly. Yet once the words had come out, he could not take them back without lying. "I said some of us are changing."

Anthony looked at him carefully. "You mean you?"

Paul let out a slow breath. "Yes."

Leonard pushed back from the table. "I knew it."

Paul's face flushed. "Knew what?"

"I knew this whole thing was getting to you," Leonard said. "First you started defending Carter. Then Whitaker. Then Jesus. Now the resurrection. You came in here an atheist, and now you are letting them talk you into faith."

Paul's eyes sharpened, not with anger exactly, but with the strain of a man tired of pretending he was unaffected. "No one talked me into anything. That is what bothers me. I wanted them to be wrong. I wanted the arguments to be weak. I wanted faith to be what I always thought it was, emotion dressed up as certainty. That is not what happened."

Leonard laughed bitterly. "You sound converted already."

Paul looked down at his notebook. "I do not know what I am."

The answer was quiet enough that Leonard did not immediately respond. Paul continued, no longer looking at Leonard but at the table in front of him. "I know what I was. I was certain God did not exist. I was certain Christianity was legend. I was certain intelligent people only believed because they needed comfort, community, or something to give life meaning. I thought I had rejected Christianity because I had outgrown it. Sitting here, listening to the evidence, I realized I rejected a version of it I never actually examined."

Rebecca Collins watched him with wide eyes. "What do you believe now?"

Paul gave a small, helpless smile. "I believe I was wrong to dismiss it."

Sheila's eyes softened. "That is not a small thing."

"No," Paul said. "It is not. I think I believe God may be real. Saying that feels strange. It feels like I am betraying myself, but maybe the self I am betraying was built on assumptions I never questioned."

The room was silent. Harold Bennett looked down at the table, not wanting to seize the moment or make Paul feel cornered. Denise Walker wiped at one eye and turned slightly away. Maria looked at Paul with the sober expression of someone watching a person step onto unfamiliar ground. Leonard stood before anyone could respond.

"I need air."

Frank looked toward the closed door. "We cannot leave without the bailiff."

"Then I need space."

Leonard moved toward the far wall, though the room was too small to provide much. His back turned toward them, but his shoulders were tight. When he spoke again, his voice was lower. "You people do not understand what this costs."

Anthony looked up sharply. He knew that tone. "What costs?"

Leonard turned around. "Letting it be true."

No one spoke.

Leonard looked at Paul, but his anger had shifted. It was no longer aimed only at him. "You think I do not know what it means if God is real? You think I have not thought about it? If God is real, then where was He? Where was He when my mother cried in the bathroom with the water running so nobody could hear? Where was He when my father stood in church with his Bible and everyone praised him? Where was He when I sat there every Sunday hoping somebody would notice something was wrong?"

His voice cracked on the last words, and he hated it. The room held still around him.

"If God is not real, then my father was just a cruel man in a cruel world," Leonard said. "I can live with that. I hate it, but I can live with it. If God is real, then I have to ask why He let that man use His name and get away with it."

Anthony's eyes had gone red. He leaned forward, elbows on his knees. "That is what I feel about my brother."

Leonard looked at him, surprised by the quiet agreement.

Anthony continued, his voice rough. "I have spent years telling myself I hated religion because of what happened to him. Maybe I do. But when this evidence started getting harder to dismiss, I got angry. Not because I was sure it was false. Because part of me was afraid it might be true. If it is true, then I have questions I do not know how to ask without screaming."

Denise let the silence breathe before she spoke. "I think God can handle screaming."

Anthony looked at her. "That is easy to say."

"No," Denise said. "It is not. I have screamed. Not always out loud. Sometimes in my car after a shift. Sometimes in the hospital chapel when I thought no one was there. I have asked God why some people die and others walk out. I have asked why children suffer. I have asked why prayers seem to go unanswered. I did not get all the answers. Sometimes all I found was enough strength to walk back into the room."

Evelyn Brooks pressed the tissue between her fingers. "After my husband died, I thought silence meant absence. I am not sure anymore."

Everyone turned toward her.

Evelyn looked embarrassed by the attention, but she did not retreat. "I have been angry for a long time. Not loudly. I am not like Leonard." She gave him a gentle glance. "I went quiet. I stopped praying because I did not want to be disappointed again. But when Dr. Reynolds talked about hope when explanations fail, and when Dr. Grant talked about resurrection, something in me hurt. Not because I rejected it. Because I missed it."

Sheila leaned forward slightly. "Missed what?"

Evelyn's eyes filled. "Hope."

The word stayed in the room without becoming a slogan. It belonged to her. No one tried to take it from her. Rebecca Collins lowered her pen. She had been the youngest voice in the room, often asking questions the others were too proud or too wounded to ask. Now her voice trembled slightly.

"I do not know how people do this," Rebecca said. "I do not know how you go from evidence to belief. I do not know what that moment is supposed to feel like."

Harold answered gently. "Most of the time it does not feel like a moment. It feels like a door opening that you did not know was closed."

Rebecca looked at him. "And then what?"

"Then you decide whether to walk through."

Rebecca's eyes moved to Paul, then to Anthony, then to Leonard. "I think mine is opening."

Paul closed his eyes briefly. The words affected him more than he expected.

Leonard shook his head, but not with the same force. "You do not even know what you believe."

Rebecca nodded. "You are right. I do not. But I know I do not believe what I believed when we came into this room. I thought Christianity was just a private religion some people needed. Now I think it might be about something that actually happened. If it happened, then I cannot treat it like a preference."

Maria felt the weight of that. She had spent years teaching students to follow evidence without being afraid of where it led, but she realized she had often kept faith in a separate room from history. The trial had opened that room.

"I think that is what has been happening to me too," Maria said. "I have always believed in God in a general way. I prayed sometimes. I believed there was meaning. But I kept Jesus at a distance. Teaching history makes you careful. You learn how traditions develop, how communities remember, how stories are shaped. That caution is good. Maybe I used caution as a way to avoid being confronted."

Harold looked at her with interest. "By Jesus?"

Maria nodded. "Yes. By Jesus. A historical figure can be studied. A risen Lord has to be answered."

Anthony stood again, though this time he did not pace. He simply seemed unable to remain seated. "I do not like that phrase."

Sheila looked at him. "What phrase?"

"Risen Lord," Anthony said. "It feels too big. Too churchy. Too much like people telling me what I have to believe. But I keep thinking about my brother. He did not need a theory. He needed someone stronger than what happened to him. I do not know why God did not stop it. I do not know why God does not stop a lot of things. But if Jesus rose from the dead, then maybe evil is not as permanent as it feels."

Denise wiped her eyes. "No, it is not."

Anthony looked at her. "I said maybe."

"I heard you."

Paul gave a small laugh, though it nearly broke. "Maybe is becoming dangerous in this room."

That brought a faint smile from Rebecca, and even Leonard looked as though he wanted to reject the humor but did not have the strength. Frank sat back and let the conversation move. He was the foreman, but he understood that pushing too soon would cheapen what was happening. The law still mattered. The verdict still mattered. They had to return to the question of Professor Price. Before they could decide what he had done, several of them were being forced to decide what the evidence had done to them.

Patricia Nguyen, who had remained composed through most of deliberations, finally spoke in a voice softer than usual. "I am Buddhist, at least culturally. My parents raised me with reverence, discipline, and respect for spiritual things. I do not come to this with hostility toward religion. But I also do not come as a Christian. What has struck me is that Christianity is making a historical claim in a way I did not expect. It is not only teaching wisdom or morality. It is saying something happened in history that changes the meaning of everything."

She looked down at her organized notes, as if for once the columns were not enough. "I am not ready to call myself converted. But I am not outside the question anymore."

Marcus Reed nodded slowly. "That may be where a lot of us are."

Leonard returned to his chair. He looked exhausted, and the anger that usually fueled him had begun to look like grief with nowhere to go. "I do not want to be inside the question."

Paul looked at him. "Neither do I."

Leonard stared at him for a long moment. "You really think you might believe?"

Paul swallowed. "I think I already believe more than I want to."

No one moved.

"I do not have all the answers," Paul said. "I do not know what to do with suffering. I do not know what to do with hypocrisy. I do not know what to do with the parts of Christianity I still do not understand. But I think God is real. And I think Jesus is not just a teacher."

Sheila closed her eyes, but she did not speak. Harold lowered his head slightly. Anthony looked away, visibly shaken. Rebecca began to cry quietly and wiped her face as if embarrassed by her own reaction. Leonard's face tightened again.

"So that is it?" Leonard asked. "You are a Christian now?"

Paul looked down at his hands. "I do not know if I know how to say that yet."

Harold raised his head. "You do not have to say more than you know."

Paul nodded, grateful. "But I think I have spent years demanding evidence from God while refusing to admit evidence when it came. If Jesus rose, then my problem is not lack of evidence. My problem is surrender."

The word landed harder than he intended. Surrender was not a courtroom word. It was not a scientific word. It was not a comfortable word for a man who had built his identity on control.

Anthony sat down slowly. "That is the part I cannot do."

Paul looked at him. "I know."

Anthony's voice dropped. "I do not know how to trust a God who let my brother get hurt."

Sheila answered with visible tenderness. "Then maybe the first step is not pretending you trust Him. Maybe the first step is telling the truth."

Anthony's eyes filled, and for once he did not cover it with a joke. "The truth is I am angry."

"Then start there," Sheila said.

"The truth is I want Him to be real and I do not want Him to be real."

Sheila nodded. "That is honest."

Leonard stared at Sheila. "And what about me?"

She looked at him. "What is the truth?"

His jaw worked for a moment before the words came. "The truth is I hate my father. And I hate that part of me still wants God to be better than him."

The room absorbed the confession with care.

Harold's voice was steady. "God is better than him."

Leonard's eyes flashed, but the anger did not fully rise. "You believe that."

"I do."

Leonard looked down at the table. "I wish I did."

It was the closest thing to a prayer Leonard had ever spoken, though he would have denied it if anyone said so. Frank finally leaned forward. He did not want to interrupt what had happened, but he knew they needed to remember why they were there.

"We need to remember why we are here," Frank said. "We are not rendering a verdict on our own souls, even if the evidence has touched them. We are deciding whether Professor Price acted improperly, whether he had a reasonable basis for his conclusions, and whether he had the right to present those conclusions as part of academic inquiry."

No one argued.

Frank continued. "I think what has happened in this room matters because it shows that the evidence is not empty. It is not shallow. It is not nonsense. It has challenged every kind of person at this table: believers, skeptics, wounded people, religious people, nonreligious people, and people who did not know what they were."

Maria nodded. "That is true."

Patricia looked across her notes. "Then maybe the question is no longer whether Professor Price's conclusions were religious. They were. The question is whether they were supported by evidence serious enough to discuss."

Marcus answered first. "They were."

Denise nodded. "Yes."

Evelyn wiped her eyes. "I believe they were."

Rebecca spoke quietly. "I do too."

Anthony hesitated, then nodded once. "I do not like all of it. But yes."

Paul looked at Frank. "Yes."

All eyes shifted toward Leonard, though no one asked him to answer immediately. He looked around the room, seeing not opponents but people who had been wounded, challenged, and changed in ways none of them had expected. His eyes moved to Paul, then Anthony, then Evelyn, then Rebecca. Something in his face softened, and for a moment he looked much younger than he was.

"I still have questions."

Harold answered gently. "So do I."

Leonard looked at him, surprised. "You?"

"Yes," Harold said. "Faith does not mean I have no questions."

Leonard sat with that. Finally he said, "Then yes. The evidence was serious enough to discuss."

The room seemed to exhale, though no one spoke of victory. It did not feel like a side had won. It felt more like the evidence had crossed a threshold and found each of them in places they had not intended to expose. Frank nodded, but he did not call for a final vote. The day had gone too far and too deep for that. Whatever verdict they reached needed to come from clear minds, not from exhaustion, emotion, or the strange momentum of a room where hearts had been opened before anyone was ready.

Paul opened his notebook one more time and looked at the sentence that had frightened him earlier. If He rose, what does that require of me? He stared at it until the words blurred slightly, then took his pen and wrote beneath it a single word that felt more like confession than conclusion.

Everything.

He closed the notebook before anyone could see what he had written.

Frank looked at the clock on the wall. It was later than he realized. The afternoon had disappeared into testimony, arguments, confessions, and questions none of them could easily put away. He rubbed his eyes and let out a slow breath.

"I do not think we should vote today," he said.

Leonard looked up, surprised. "Why not?"

"Because we are tired," Frank said. "And because too much has happened in this room. We owe Professor Price a verdict based on judgment, not exhaustion."

Maria nodded. "I agree."

Patricia gathered the loose pages in front of her and tapped them into order. "So tomorrow morning?"

Frank looked around the table. "Tomorrow morning. We come back, review the legal question, and vote."

No one objected. Even Leonard remained quiet.

A knock came at the door a few minutes later, and the bailiff stepped in. Judge Hayes had recessed for the day. The jurors were reminded not to discuss the case with anyone, not to read or watch anything related to the trial, and not to form a final verdict until deliberations resumed. They had heard the warning before, but that evening it sounded different. The case was no longer something they could leave neatly inside the courthouse.

One by one, they gathered their belongings. Maria closed her notebook and held it against her chest for a moment before placing it in her bag. Denise folded her scarf with unnecessary care. Patricia secured her papers in perfect order, though her hands moved more slowly than usual. Anthony slipped his phone into his pocket but did not check it. Evelyn stood carefully, as though the day had made her older. Rebecca wiped beneath one eye and pretended she was only tired.

Paul remained seated until most of the others had stood. When he finally rose, he kept his notebook pressed under his arm like it contained something dangerous. Leonard was the last to move. He stood by the window in the door for a few seconds, looking into the hallway. No one rushed him. When he turned back toward the table, his eyes briefly met Harold's.

"I still do not know what I believe," Leonard said.

Harold picked up his coat. "Neither did Thomas at first."

Leonard's face tightened, but there was less anger in it than before. "Do not preach at me."

Harold gave a faint smile. "I was not. I was just telling you that questions do not disqualify a man."

Leonard looked away, but he did not argue.

The bailiff led them out of the deliberation room and down the courthouse hallway. The building had grown quieter with the evening. Earlier in the trial, reporters had crowded the corridors, waiting for statements, reactions, and any hint of movement. Now most of them had gone. Only a few remained near the exit, speaking in low voices and watching the jurors with the restrained hunger of people trained to notice everything.

The jurors did not speak as they walked. The sound of their shoes against the polished floor filled the silence. They passed the courtroom doors, now closed and dark through the narrow glass panels. Inside that room, witnesses had answered questions under oath, attorneys had argued, objections had been raised, and the public had watched the case as if it belonged to the nation. The hardest work had not happened under the lights or before the cameras. It had happened in the smaller room behind the jury box, where twelve people had been forced to examine not only the evidence, but themselves.

Outside the courthouse, the evening air felt cooler than expected. The sky over the city had begun to darken, and traffic moved beyond the courthouse steps with ordinary indifference. People were going home from work, stopping for groceries, answering messages, and thinking about dinner. Life had continued while the jurors sat in a room asking whether God could be dismissed as private opinion.

They separated slowly. Maria walked toward the parking garage with her notebook in her bag and the image of the man from Nazareth fixed in her thoughts. Denise stood near the curb for a moment before calling for a ride, her mind already returning to hospital rooms and prayers whispered beside bedsides. Anthony headed toward his truck but stopped twice before reaching it, as if he had forgotten where he parked or what he was supposed to do next. Evelyn held her purse close and looked up at the evening sky longer than necessary.

Rebecca Collins called her roommate and said she was fine, though her voice suggested otherwise. Patricia sat in her car without starting the engine, staring at the steering wheel while her neatly organized notes rested on the passenger seat. Frank walked to his vehicle with the slow pace of a man who knew tomorrow's vote would be easier than what had already taken place. Paul reached his car and stood beside it for several seconds, unable to open the door. He could still feel the weight of the notebook under his arm.

Leonard crossed the parking lot alone. He did not look back at the courthouse. He did not want to think about Harold's words, Paul's change, Anthony's grief, or the possibility that the God he had rejected might not resemble the father who had taught him to hate religion. He wanted the anger back. Anger was familiar. Anger did not ask him to forgive, reconsider, or hope.

As he reached his truck, he found himself remembering his mother in the bathroom with the water running. For the first time in years, he wondered whether she had been praying. The courthouse doors closed behind them as evening settled over the city. Tomorrow they would return to decide the case. Tonight, each of them would go home to face what the case had uncovered.

# 22

By the time Paul Jensen reached his apartment, the city had settled into the ordinary sounds of evening. A dog barked somewhere beyond the parking lot. A neighbor's television murmured through a shared wall, and someone upstairs dragged a chair across the floor. None of it should have felt strange, but everything did. The world had continued as though nothing had happened, as though twelve jurors had not spent the day arguing over suffering, resurrection, and the possibility that God had stepped into history.

Paul unlocked his door and stepped inside. His apartment was clean in the way a man keeps things clean when he lives alone and does not want disorder accusing him. A laptop sat closed on the kitchen table, and a row of technical books lined a shelf near the window. There were no crosses on the walls, no family Bible on the coffee table, and no signs that religion had ever occupied the place. That had always suited him. He preferred spaces without symbols because symbols asked too much.

He set his keys in the bowl by the door and placed his notebook on the table. For several minutes, he stood there looking at it as if it might open by itself. He thought about turning on the television, but Judge Hayes's instruction returned immediately. No news. No commentary. No outside information. He thought about opening his laptop and searching the questions that had followed him home, but that too felt like crossing a line. He was still a juror, and he owed the case discipline even if his own soul felt undisciplined.

He walked to the sink, filled a glass of water, and drank half of it without tasting anything. Then he sat down at the table and opened his notebook to the page he had tried not to think about. If He rose, what does that require of me? Everything. The word looked foreign in his handwriting. Paul read it once, then again, as though repeated exposure might make it less threatening. It did not.

He leaned back and covered his face with both hands. He did not know how to pray, and that embarrassed him, though there was no one in the room to see it. Prayer had always seemed to him like speaking into the dark and calling the echo God. Now, for the first time in years, the silence did not feel empty. It felt occupied. He lowered his hands and stared at the ceiling.

"If You're there," he said, his voice barely louder than breath, "I don't know what I'm doing."

The words sounded foolish in the room. He almost laughed at himself, but the laugh caught somewhere in his chest.

"I don't know how to believe," he said. "I don't know what changes. I don't even know if this is real or if I'm just tired. But if Jesus rose from the dead, then I can't pretend I didn't hear it."

He stopped, unsettled by the sound of his own confession. No light filled the room. No voice answered him. The refrigerator hummed, a car passed outside, and the neighbor's television continued murmuring through the wall. Nothing happened that could be mistaken for proof. Still, Paul did not feel alone.

Across town, Leonard Shaw sat in his truck long after pulling into his driveway. The porch light had burned out three weeks earlier, and he had not replaced it. In the darkness, the house looked smaller than usual, tired and waiting. He gripped the steering wheel and told himself he was angry about the trial. That was easier than admitting the truth. The trial had gone home with him because it had found things he had buried under years of sarcasm, work, and stubborn unbelief.

He finally got out and entered the house. The air inside smelled faintly of dust, old wood, and the microwave dinner he had eaten the night before. He dropped his keys on the counter and went straight to the refrigerator, but after opening it, he realized he was not hungry. He closed it again and stood in the kitchen with one hand still on the handle. His mother's face came to him without warning, not the face from photographs, but the face from memory.

She stood at the bathroom sink, dabbing makeup under one eye while the water ran hard enough to cover the sound of her crying. He had been twelve, old enough to know something was wrong and too young to do anything about it. His father had already left for men's breakfast at the church, carrying his Bible under one arm. Leonard could still remember the smell of aftershave in the hallway and the silence that followed the closing of the front door. He had hated that silence then. He hated it more now.

Leonard walked to the small hallway closet and opened the door. He did not know why. Inside were paint cans, a toolbox, an old vacuum cleaner, and a cardboard box he had brought from his mother's house after she died. He had never fully unpacked it. He pulled it out and set it on the kitchen table.

For a while, he only looked at the box. Then he opened it. There were old envelopes, a chipped ceramic angel, photographs, a folded scarf, and a Bible with a cracked brown cover. Leonard stared at it. He had not seen it in years, but he knew it immediately. His mother had carried it to church every Sunday. His father had carried his own Bible in public, but this one had lived beside her bed.

Leonard did not open it at first. He told himself he had no reason to. He was not going to violate the judge's order by studying religion during deliberations. He was not going to let the case turn his house into a chapel. But he did not have to open it to remember her hands on the cover. He sat down slowly.

"Why didn't you leave him?" he asked the empty kitchen.

No answer came, but the question had never truly been for her. It had always been for God, though Leonard had spent decades pretending otherwise. His phone buzzed, and he looked at the screen. A text from his sister, Carla, waited there.

Everything okay? Saw trial on news but didn't watch. Thinking of you.

Leonard stared at the message. He typed, Fine, then deleted it. He typed, Long day, then deleted that too. Finally, he set the phone down without answering. He looked back at the Bible, his throat tightening before he could stop it.

"I wish You were better than him," he whispered.

The words startled him. He had not meant to say them. He pushed the chair back and stood quickly, as if distance from the table might give him distance from the confession. But the sentence remained in the room, and the room did not let him take it back.

At his restaurant, Anthony Russo sat alone in a booth near the back while two employees cleaned the kitchen. Russo's had been his father's dream before it became his, and most nights the noise of the place comforted him. Pans clattered, orders were called, and customers laughed over plates of pasta and garlic bread. The restaurant gave him something religion never had. It gave him a place where hard work produced something visible.

That night, the dining room had emptied, and the silence pressed on him. His younger brother, Michael, came through the side door carrying a plastic container of leftover bread. He was forty-three now, but Anthony still saw him as the boy he had once been: thin, nervous, and always watching adults too carefully. The abuse had taken place when Michael was twelve. The family had discovered it too late, and the church had handled it the way institutions sometimes handle evil, with quiet meetings, careful statements, and more concern for scandal than for the wounded.

Michael stopped when he saw Anthony sitting in the booth. "You look like somebody died."

Anthony forced a smile. "Long day."

Michael slid into the booth across from him. "Jury stuff?"

Anthony looked toward the kitchen, making sure no one was close enough to hear. "I can't talk about the case."

"I know." Michael leaned back and studied him. "But you can talk about you."

Anthony looked down at his hands. They were broad, scarred by burns and knife cuts from years in kitchens. "Do you ever pray anymore?"

Michael's face changed. The question had crossed a line neither of them usually approached. "Sometimes."

Anthony looked up. "After everything?"

Michael nodded slowly. "After everything."

Anthony felt irritation rise, then guilt for feeling it. "How?"

Michael glanced toward the dark windows facing the street. "I don't know if I can explain it. For a long time, I thought God was locked inside that building with the man who hurt me. I couldn't separate them. Every hymn, every collar, every prayer sounded like him."

Anthony watched him, saying nothing.

"Then one day I realized something," Michael continued. "If Jesus is who they said He is, then that man didn't represent Him. He betrayed Him."

Anthony stared at him. The words were too close to what Harold had said in the jury room, and he resented the way they followed him home. "That's what people keep saying."

"Maybe because it's true."

Anthony's jaw tightened. "Don't do that."

"I'm not preaching to you," Michael said. "You asked."

Anthony looked away.

Michael's voice softened. "I still get angry. I still have memories. God didn't erase them. But I don't think the man who hurt me gets to define God forever."

Anthony swallowed. "I don't know how you do that."

"Some days I don't."

The honesty disarmed him more than certainty would have. Anthony sat back in the booth, listening to the muffled sounds of the kitchen, and realized that for years he had defended his brother by rejecting everything connected to God. His brother had not asked him to do that. Maybe Anthony's hatred of religion had become another room where the abuser still controlled the furniture.

He rubbed both hands over his face. "I don't want to forgive that man."

Michael's eyes darkened. "I didn't ask you to."

"I don't want God to ask me either."

Michael looked at him for a long moment. "Maybe start by asking God what He thinks about what happened."

Anthony gave a bitter laugh. "I already know what I think."

"I know," Michael said. "But maybe you need to know what He thinks."

Anthony had no answer. For once, his anger did not feel strong. It felt tired.

Evelyn Brooks returned to a house that had been quiet for so long she had stopped noticing the silence. Her husband's coat still hung in the hall closet, not because she believed he would return for it, but because removing it had felt too final. She made tea, forgot to drink it, and wandered into the living room where his chair sat near the window. For thirty years, she had passed that chair with the practiced strength of a widow who had learned to live around absence. That night, she sat in it.

The chair creaked under her weight. It still seemed shaped for him, though the fabric had faded and the armrests had worn smooth. She ran her fingers along the seam and remembered the night he died, the hospital lights, the doctor speaking gently, and the pastor arriving too late with words that sounded rehearsed. She had not blamed the pastor. Not really. But his attempts to explain what could not be explained had made her grief feel crowded.

She looked toward the small table beside the chair. A framed photograph of her husband smiled back at her from a summer thirty-five years gone. She lifted the frame and held it against her chest.

"I missed hope," she said aloud.

The sentence came with tears. She did not fight them. She was too old and too tired to be embarrassed by grief in an empty room. When the crying slowed, she looked toward the ceiling, then closed her eyes.

"God," she whispered, and the name felt strange from disuse. "I don't know if I am ready to come back. I don't know if I know how. But if You have been here, and I have been the one turned away, help me turn around."

She sat in the chair until the tea in the kitchen went cold.

Rebecca Collins lived with two roommates in an apartment filled with plants, art prints, mismatched furniture, and the restless energy of people still learning how to become adults. When she walked in, one roommate looked up from the couch.

"How was court?"

Rebecca set her bag down by the door. "I can't talk about it."

"I know, but are you okay?"

Rebecca opened her mouth to say yes and found she could not lie convincingly. "I don't think so."

Her roommate sat up. "Do you want to talk about something else?"

Rebecca smiled faintly. "That might be worse."

She went to her room and closed the door. Her desk was covered with sketches for freelance design work, color swatches, and half-finished ideas for a client who wanted a logo that felt modern but timeless, simple but unforgettable. Yesterday, Rebecca would have found that annoying. Tonight, it seemed almost funny that people wanted clarity from a logo when she could not find it in her own heart.

She sat on the edge of the bed and thought about Harold's words. Most of the time belief does not feel like a moment. It feels like a door opening that you did not know was closed. Rebecca had not grown up rejecting God. She had grown up without Him being presented as necessary. Religion had belonged to other families, other holidays, other people. It was not hated in her home. It was simply absent.

Her parents had taught kindness, effort, and independence, and she was grateful for that. Yet the trial had shown her that absence was not neutrality. It was a kind of inheritance too. She picked up her sketchpad and drew a door. Then she drew it slightly open, with light spilling through the gap. She stared at it for a long time, then wrote beneath it, I think mine is opening.

For the first time since deliberations began, she wondered if the ache in her chest was not fear. Maybe it was invitation.

Maria Alvarez went home to a small house filled with books. History lived everywhere in her home. Roman biographies leaned against Civil War letters. A stack of essays waited on the dining room table. A map of the ancient Mediterranean hung framed in the hallway, a gift from former students who knew her too well. She dropped her bag near the door and stood before the map.

Her eyes went instinctively to Judea. She had pointed to that region countless times in classrooms, describing empires, revolts, trade routes, sects, governors, religious tensions, and the machinery of Rome. She had taught Jesus as a figure of history, careful to maintain academic distance. She had always believed that caution made her fair. Tonight, she wondered if caution had also made her safe.

Her daughter called while Maria was still standing in the hallway. "Mom, are you okay? You sound tired."

"I am tired."

"Jury duty?"

"Yes."

"Can you talk about it?"

"No."

"Is it hard?"

Maria looked at the map. "Harder than I expected."

Her daughter was quiet for a moment. "You always tell your students history matters because real people lived it."

Maria smiled faintly. "I do say that."

"Maybe remember that."

After they hung up, Maria stayed in the hall. A historical figure could be studied. A risen Lord had to be answered. She had said that in the jury room, and now the sentence stood before her in her own house, refusing to behave like a line from someone else's testimony.

Patricia Nguyen sat in her car for nearly fifteen minutes after reaching home. The garage light had gone off twice, and twice she waved one hand to trigger it again. Her notes sat on the passenger seat, neatly clipped and arranged. Order had always comforted her. Numbers balanced. Ledgers reconciled. Facts could be categorized. Questions could be placed in columns. The trial had not respected her columns.

When she finally entered the house, her mother was in the kitchen washing herbs. The smell of ginger and garlic filled the room.

"You are late," her mother said.

"Long day."

"You ate?"

"Not really."

Her mother dried her hands and studied her daughter with the quiet authority of a woman who noticed more than she said. "Something is heavy."

Patricia set her bag on a chair. "I can't talk about the case."

"I did not ask about the case."

Patricia smiled wearily. "No. I guess you didn't."

Her mother placed a bowl of soup on the table and sat across from her. Patricia ate because refusing would have required more energy than she had. The warmth helped. So did the silence. After a while, Patricia looked toward the small shelf in the corner where her mother kept incense, family photographs, and symbols of reverence that had shaped Patricia's childhood.

"Mom, do you think truth can come from outside what we were taught?"

Her mother did not seem surprised by the question. "If it is truth, it is not afraid of where it is found."

Patricia looked at her. "Even if it changes you?"

Her mother smiled gently. "Especially then."

Patricia lowered her eyes. She was not ready to call herself Christian. She was not ready to abandon the reverence that had shaped her family. But she was beginning to understand that truth was not a possession passed down unchanged. It was something that could confront every tradition, including her own.

Denise Walker drove past the hospital on her way home and pulled into the parking lot before she fully decided to stop. She no longer worked night shifts regularly, but the building still felt like another home, one built of fluorescent light, grief, antiseptic, and courage. She sat in the parking lot for several minutes, watching people move through the sliding doors. Inside that building, prayers were being prayed at that very moment. Some would be answered with recovery. Some would end in funerals. Denise had lived long enough not to offer cheap certainty about either.

She did not go inside. Instead, she remained in the car and thought of the children she had cared for, the parents she had held, the patients who had whispered that they were afraid, and the families who asked whether God heard them. She had always said yes. Some days she believed it with fire. Other days she believed it with the last thread of strength she had left.

Her phone buzzed with a message from a former colleague.

Rough day here. Pray if you can.

Denise closed her eyes. "Lord, be near," she whispered.

It was not a long prayer, but it was the only one she had strength for. As she sat there, she realized that the trial had not weakened her faith. It had stripped away the easy parts and left something quieter, deeper, and less afraid of questions.

Frank Dawson arrived home to find his wife, Ellen, reading at the kitchen table. She looked up when he entered and immediately closed the book.

"You look worn out."

Frank set his keys on the counter. "I am."

"Can you talk about it?"

"No."

She nodded. They had been married long enough to understand the difference between privacy and distance.

"Then sit down."

He did. She placed a cup of decaf in front of him and sat across from him without asking another question. Frank loved her for that. He had spent the day guiding a room full of people through arguments that had become confessions. At home, he had no strength left to guide anything.

After a long silence, he said, "Have I changed?"

Ellen studied him. "Since when?"

"Since this trial started."

She smiled softly. "You've become quieter."

"That does not sound like a compliment."

"It is from me."

Frank looked at the steam rising from his cup. "I thought this would be about facts."

"Isn't it?"

"It is," he said. "But facts do things to people when they matter."

Ellen reached across the table and rested her hand over his. "Then let them do what they need to do."

Frank nodded, though he was not sure whether she meant the other jurors or him.

Marcus Reed went home to an empty apartment and a stack of cold case files he had promised himself he would not touch that night. He touched them anyway. The top file concerned a young woman whose killer had never been found. Her mother's letters were still inside, each one asking if there had been progress. Marcus had answered every letter with professionalism. He had never told her that some cases followed detectives home and aged with them.

He sat at the kitchen table and opened the file. The evidence was familiar: photographs, timelines, interviews, lab reports, and dead ends. He thought about justice. He thought about the families who never received it. He thought about Dr. Avery admitting that without God there was no final reckoning. Marcus had not considered himself religious in any serious way. He believed in law, evidence, and the hard work of finding truth in a world where people lied.

But law was limited. Evidence disappeared. Witnesses died. Guilty people walked free. If this life was the only courtroom, too many cases ended unresolved. He closed the file. For the first time in years, he hoped there was another Judge beyond the ones he had known.

Harold Bennett did not turn on the lights when he entered his house. He stood in the dim entryway for a moment, listening to the quiet. His wife had died six years earlier, and although he had built routines around the absence, there were evenings when the silence still surprised him. He walked into the living room and sat in the chair where he prayed each morning. He did not pray immediately.

Instead, he thought about Paul, Anthony, Leonard, Rebecca, Evelyn, and the way the evidence had moved through the room like a plow turning hard ground. When he finally bowed his head, his prayer was simple.

"Lord, do not let me get in the way."

He meant it. He had seen Christians ruin holy moments by trying to manage them. He had no desire to win arguments if winning meant bruising people God was already drawing.

Sheila Morrison stood in her kitchen washing a mug that was already clean. She had spent her life helping children find words for things they could not yet understand. That day in the jury room, she had seen adults in the same condition. Anthony had anger. Leonard had hatred. Rebecca had confusion. Paul had surrender pressing at the edges of his reason. Evelyn had grief. Each of them had spoken like someone standing near a door, afraid of what might happen if it opened.

Her husband called from the living room. "You all right?"

She set the mug in the drainer. "Yes."

"You sure?"

She smiled, though he could not see it. "No."

He appeared in the doorway. "Can you tell me?"

She shook her head. "Not yet."

He understood. He came over, kissed her forehead, and left her alone. Sheila held the edge of the counter and prayed without closing her eyes.

"Jesus, be gentle with them."

It was the prayer of a woman who had learned that truth could be firm without being cruel.

By midnight, the jurors were scattered across the city, each in a different room, each facing a different version of the same question. The court had instructed them not to discuss the case, and they obeyed. No instruction could stop the evidence from speaking inside them. It followed Paul into the silence of his apartment. It sat with Leonard beside his mother's Bible. It met Anthony in the back booth of his restaurant. It found Evelyn in her husband's chair, Rebecca in front of a sketch of an open door, Maria before a map of Judea, Patricia at her mother's kitchen table, Denise outside the hospital, Marcus beside an old case file, Frank across from the woman who knew him best, Harold in prayer, and Sheila at her sink whispering for mercy.

Tomorrow they would return to the courthouse. Tomorrow they would vote. Before they judged the case, each of them had to spend one night alone with what the truth had uncovered.

# 23

THE NEXT MORNING ARRIVED with a quiet that felt different from every other morning of the trial. The jurors entered the courthouse one by one, each carrying Judge Hayes's instruction not to speak about the case and the heavier burden of knowing that silence had not stopped the case from speaking to them. They had gone home as jurors, but most of them had returned with the private awareness that the trial had followed them into kitchens, bedrooms, empty houses, hospital parking lots, restaurants, and memories they had not expected to revisit. The courthouse looked the same, the security line moved with the same practiced routine, and the hallway outside Courtroom One held the same polished stillness. Yet nothing felt the same to the twelve people who would soon decide the case.

Frank Dawson was the first to reach the deliberation room. He set his coat over the back of his chair, placed his yellow legal pad in front of him, and waited. He had slept only a few hours, but his mind was clearer than it had been when they left the courthouse the evening before. That was why he had refused to vote the previous day. Emotion had filled the room, and although emotion did not make their conclusions false, it could make them careless. Professor Price deserved better than a verdict made in exhaustion.

Maria Alvarez entered next, holding her notebook close to her chest. She gave Frank a small nod and took her seat. Patricia Nguyen followed, her papers in perfect order, though the look in her eyes suggested that order on the page had not brought order to her thoughts. Denise Walker came in quietly, then Evelyn Brooks, who seemed both tired and strangely peaceful. Rebecca Collins arrived with her sketchpad tucked beneath her notebook, its cover pressed tightly against her side.

Anthony Russo entered with his hands in his pockets, his usual humor absent. He gave no greeting beyond a slight lift of his chin. Marcus Reed came in behind him and sat with the posture of a man ready to work through the facts one final time. Harold Bennett and Sheila Morrison entered together but did not speak as they took their seats. The room filled slowly, each arrival adding to the silence rather than breaking it.

Paul Jensen arrived near the end, carrying the same notebook he had held against his chest the evening before. He looked different to several of them, though no one could have said exactly how. His face was pale, and the sharp certainty that had defined him at the beginning of deliberations had been replaced by something quieter and more exposed. He sat down without opening the notebook. Whatever he had written inside it had already followed him into the room.

Leonard Shaw came in last. He closed the door behind him and stood there for a moment with one hand still on the knob. His eyes moved around the room, passing over each face before settling briefly on Harold. He looked as though he had slept poorly, if he had slept at all. His jaw was set, but the old defiance no longer seemed to come as easily. After a moment, he took his seat.

Frank waited until everyone was settled. "Before we vote," he said, "I think we need to remind ourselves of the legal question. We are not deciding whether every one of us believes in God. We are not deciding whether every one of us accepts Christianity. We are not deciding whether Professor Price answered every objection. The question is whether he acted improperly by presenting his conclusions as something that could be examined through evidence, reason, history, morality, and inquiry."

No one interrupted him.

Frank looked down at the notes he had written over the last two days. The phrases were still there, but he did not read them dramatically. He treated them like work notes, because that was what they had become. "We said there was reasonable disagreement concerning the beginning of the universe. We said the source of morality was disputed but serious. We said suffering remained unresolved but had not been ignored. We said Jesus existed historically and that His meaning was disputed. We said His claims were serious and could not be reduced to simple moral teaching. We said the resurrection argument was not blind faith, even for those who did not accept it."

Leonard leaned back but said nothing.

Frank continued. "The issue before us is whether a professor may follow that evidence to a conclusion, state that conclusion honestly, and allow students to challenge it. That is what we need to vote on."

Maria opened her notebook, though she seemed to know her thoughts without needing the page. "I think he may. As a teacher, I care about the classroom. I care about students not being pressured. I care about inquiry remaining open. If Professor Price had punished students for disagreeing, that would be different. If he had hidden opposing views, that would be different. The testimony did not show that. It showed that he presented a conclusion and invited examination. I may not agree with every conclusion he reached, but I cannot say he acted outside honest academic inquiry."

Patricia rested both hands on her carefully stacked notes. "I agree. I approached this by listing what the witnesses conceded. Again and again, Northbridge's witnesses disagreed with interpretation but accepted many of the facts. That matters. Professor Price was not inventing evidence. He was interpreting evidence. I am not a Christian, and I am not ready to accept everything he believes, but I believe his conclusions were supported enough to be discussed seriously."

Marcus nodded as if Patricia had summarized the case the way he would have summarized an investigation. "For me, this came down to evidence and explanation. In my work, people can disagree over what the evidence means. That does not make one side dishonest. Professor Price put forward a case. The university may disagree with it, students may challenge it, other professors may reject it, but disagreement is not misconduct. I vote in favor of Professor Price."

Denise looked down at her notes before speaking. Her eyes were tired, but her voice was steady. "I struggled most with suffering. I still do. I have spent too many years beside hospital beds to pretend faith answers every question neatly. Professor

Price did not pretend that. His witnesses did not pretend that. What I saw was not blind faith refusing pain, but faith willing to face pain. That is not misconduct. That is courage. My vote is for Professor Price."

Evelyn Brooks looked down at the tissue folded in her hand, then placed it beside her notebook. "I had stopped believing that faith had anything to say to grief. I am not saying I have everything settled after this trial. I do not. But I know the testimony was serious. It deserved to be heard. Professor Price did not force anyone to believe. He asked questions that many of us had stopped asking. I vote in his favor."

Rebecca Collins swallowed, looking younger than she had on the first day of deliberations. "I came into this with almost no religious background. I thought religion was mostly private, like personal taste or family tradition. After listening to the witnesses and after hearing everyone in this room, I do not think that anymore. I do not know exactly what I believe yet. But I know Professor Price was not making empty claims. He had reasons. He had evidence. He should not be punished for presenting them."

Anthony rubbed his hands together and stared at the tabletop for a long moment before speaking. When he finally looked up, his expression was unguarded in a way none of them had seen on the first day. "I still have trouble with religion. I want that on the table. I have seen the damage it can do when the wrong people use it. I still do not know what to do with that."

He paused, and no one rushed him.

"But Professor Price is not the man who hurt my brother," Anthony said. "The evidence in this case is not the institution that protected evil. I have to separate those things if I am going to be honest. I do not know if I believe the resurrection. I do not know if I trust church. But I know this case was not about whether my wounds are real. It was about whether Professor Price had the right to present evidence for what he believes is true. I think he did."

Sheila looked at Anthony with compassion but did not speak for him. He had found his own words, and that mattered. Harold Bennett sat upright, his voice calm and controlled when his turn came. "I entered this room already believing in God, so I have tried to be careful. I did not want my faith to make me unfair. But I also do not believe fairness requires pretending conviction is dangerous. Professor Price did what every honest teacher should do. He presented evidence, stated his conclusion, welcomed scrutiny, and allowed disagreement. That is not indoctrination. That is inquiry. I vote for Professor Price."

Sheila Morrison nodded. "I agree. Faith that fears questions is fragile, but what we heard in this trial was not fragile. It was examined from every side. It was pressed by science, philosophy, suffering, history, and skepticism. Professor Price's position survived enough scrutiny that no one can honestly call it reckless. I vote in his favor."

All eyes shifted toward Paul.

He had been looking down at his notebook, but he did not open it. He had written enough in it the night before. He knew what was there, and he knew what had changed inside him because of it. When he spoke, his voice was steady, though the steadiness seemed to cost him effort.

"I came into this trial as an atheist," Paul said. "I do not say that lightly, and I do not say it as a performance. I was certain. Not curious. Certain. I thought belief in God was something intelligent people outgrew. I thought Christianity was legend supported by emotion and tradition. I thought the people defending faith would have to avoid evidence in order to keep believing."

He paused and looked briefly toward Leonard, not as an opponent but as the only person in the room who might understand the cost of saying what came next. "I was wrong. I was wrong about the strength of the arguments. I was wrong about the historical evidence. I was wrong about what faith meant to the people who testified. I was wrong to dismiss what I had not examined."

No one moved.

"I do not know what label I am ready to carry today," Paul continued, "but I believe God is real in a way I did not believe when this trial began. I believe Jesus is more than a teacher. Even if I were not ready to say that, I would still vote for Professor Price because his conclusions were not blind. They were reasoned, argued, tested, and serious."

Paul looked down, visibly shaken by his own words, then closed his hands around the edge of the table. "My vote is for Professor Price."

The room remained quiet. It was not the silence of people waiting for a dramatic response. It was the silence of people recognizing that a man had just crossed a threshold in front of them and could not easily cross back. Only Leonard had not spoken. He felt the weight of their attention and hated it.

For most of his life, anger had helped him keep control of rooms. If he sounded certain enough, people backed away. If he made faith sound foolish enough, he did not have to admit how much it had once mattered. The last two days had stripped away the safety of his contempt. He could still reject God. He could still reject the church. He could still reject every conclusion Harold believed and every new question Paul had begun to ask. What he could no longer do was pretend the evidence was nothing.

Frank did not rush him.

Leonard looked toward Anthony first. "You said Professor Price is not the man who hurt your brother."

Anthony nodded. "I did."

Leonard looked toward Harold. "And you said my father betrayed the God he claimed to worship."

Harold's expression remained steady. "Yes."

Leonard swallowed, and the motion seemed to irritate him because it revealed effort. "I do not know what to do with that. I spent most of my life using my father as proof that religion was rotten. Maybe some of it is. Maybe a lot of it is. I still believe people hide behind God. I still believe churches protect men they should expose. I still believe some prayers go unanswered in ways that make no sense to me."

His voice grew rougher, but he kept going. "But last night I found my mother's Bible."

The room grew still.

"I did not read it," Leonard said. "I knew we were not supposed to study anything related to the case, and I did not. But I held it. I remembered her carrying it. I remembered her crying with the water running. For the first time in years, I wondered if maybe she was not weak for praying. Maybe she was holding on to something I never understood."

Leonard looked away from them because their faces had become too much. "I am not converted. I am not ready to forgive my father. I am not ready to say I believe the way Harold believes or the way Paul might be starting to believe. But I can say this honestly. Professor Price had evidence. He had reason. He had the right to present his conclusions. Northbridge was wrong to punish him for that."

Frank's face softened. "Is that your vote?"

Leonard nodded once. "My vote is for Professor Price."

No one spoke at first. There was no applause, no celebration, and no rush to turn the moment into triumph. The verdict had come, but it had come through too much honesty to be treated lightly. Frank looked around the table, meeting each juror's eyes one by one. Maria, Patricia, Marcus, Denise, Evelyn, Rebecca, Anthony, Harold, Sheila, Paul, Leonard. Twelve people, twelve histories, twelve sets of assumptions, wounds, convictions, and questions. The vote was unanimous.

Frank took the verdict form from the folder the bailiff had left with them. His hand was steady as he filled it out, but he felt the weight of every word. In favor of Professor Daniel Price. He signed as foreman and set the pen down.

Maria let out a breath she had been holding. "So that is it."

Frank looked at the form. "Legally, yes."

Paul gave a faint, tired smile. "That may be the easiest part."

Leonard looked at him, and for once there was no mockery in his expression. "Do not start preaching."

Paul shook his head. "I would not know how."

Anthony leaned back in his chair. "That makes two of us."

Rebecca Collins smiled through eyes that were still damp. The exchange was small, but it eased the room. After everything they had said, after the confessions and arguments and questions that had torn through them, the faint return of ordinary humor felt like mercy.

Frank stood and walked to the door. He knocked once, then waited for the bailiff.

When the door opened, the bailiff looked from Frank to the others. "Has the jury reached a verdict?"

Frank held the form in his hand. He looked back at the table one more time before answering. The jurors were no longer arguing. Some sat quietly. Some stared at the floor. Paul held his notebook closed with both hands. Leonard looked toward the window, but not with the same hardness as before. Anthony sat with his head bowed, his thumb moving slowly over his wedding ring. Evelyn's lips moved silently, though no one asked whether she was praying.

Frank turned back to the bailiff. "Yes. We have."

The bailiff nodded and stepped aside to notify the court.

The jurors gathered their belongings in near silence. They had entered the deliberation room as strangers assigned to decide a case. They would leave it having done that, but also having faced questions no verdict form could contain. The law had required them to judge whether Professor Price's conclusions deserved protection. The evidence had required something more private from each of them.

A few minutes later, the bailiff returned and told them the court was ready. Frank picked up the verdict form. The others rose with him. No one spoke as they moved toward the door. Together, they walked back toward Courtroom One.

# 24

The courtroom was already full when the bailiff opened the side door and led the jurors back to their seats. For three weeks, the nation had watched experts argue over science, morality, suffering, history, and the resurrection of Jesus Christ, but the room felt different now. The testimony was finished. The arguments were finished. Even the waiting had come to an end. What remained was a folded verdict form in the foreman's possession and twelve people who had carried the weight of the case farther than anyone in the gallery could know.

Professor Daniel Price sat at the plaintiff's table beside David Stone. He looked older than he had at the beginning of the trial. The strain of public accusation, testimony, headlines, and uncertainty had worn lines into his face that had not been there three weeks earlier. Yet there was no panic in him. He had done what he believed conscience required, he had told the truth as he understood it, and now the decision belonged to others.

David sat beside him, quiet and steady. He had not slept much the night before, but he had learned over the years that courtroom fatigue could not be allowed to guide the moment.

His duty was to remain composed, especially when the outcome mattered this much. He looked toward the jury box as the jurors took their seats. He noticed Paul first, then Leonard, then Anthony, and something in their faces told him the deliberations had gone beyond a legal discussion. They did not look like people who had merely reached a decision. They looked like people who had been reached by it.

Across the aisle, Rebecca Kane stood at the defense table, arranging papers she no longer needed to arrange. The verdict had not yet been read, but she felt as though she already knew the direction of the room. She had spent her career trusting preparation, discipline, and control. She knew how to question witnesses, expose weaknesses, narrow arguments, and frame uncertainty. What she had not prepared for was the way the trial had exposed her own uncertainty. She had defended the university with skill, but somewhere along the way, the questions had stopped belonging only to Professor Price.

Judge Eleanor Hayes entered the courtroom promptly, and everyone rose. Her expression revealed nothing. She took her seat, waited for the courtroom to settle, and looked toward the jury. The courtroom deputy stood ready near the clerk's station, and the bailiff remained beside the jury box. No one moved unnecessarily. No one wanted to be the person who broke the silence before the verdict was received.

"Ladies and gentlemen," Judge Hayes said, "I understand you have reached a verdict."

Frank Dawson stood. His face was solemn, not proud. He held the verdict form carefully, as if he understood that the paper represented more than a legal conclusion. "We have, Your Honor."

The bailiff took the form from him and carried it to the bench. Judge Hayes read it in silence. The room seemed to hold its breath without meaning to. Reporters leaned forward. Professor Price lowered his eyes. Rebecca kept her gaze fixed on the judge because she did not trust herself to look anywhere else.

After a long moment, Judge Hayes handed the form back to the clerk. "The clerk will read the verdict."

The clerk stood and unfolded the page. "In the matter of Price v. Northbridge University, on the plaintiff's claim that the university unlawfully disciplined Professor Daniel Price for academic expression protected within the bounds of inquiry, we, the jury, find in favor of the plaintiff, Professor Daniel Price."

A murmur moved through the courtroom before Judge Hayes raised her hand. It was not loud, but it was enough to remind everyone that the court was still in session.

"Order, please," Judge Hayes said.

The clerk continued. "We further find that Professor Price's conclusions, whether accepted or rejected by others, were presented as matters capable of rational and evidentiary examination, supported by evidence and argument, and open to scrutiny and disagreement. We find that disagreement with his conclusions did not constitute misconduct."

Professor Price did not move at first. He sat there with his eyes closed, as if the words had reached him more slowly than everyone else. David leaned closer and spoke quietly enough that only Price could hear him.

“It’s over,” David said.

Professor Price opened his eyes. “No,” he said softly. “But this part is.”

David understood what he meant. The trial had ended, but the questions it had raised would continue long after the courtroom emptied. For Professor Price, the verdict did not erase the cost. His reputation had been dragged into public controversy. His students had been divided. His university had turned against him. His faith had been examined under the pressure of hostile scrutiny. The jury had vindicated him, but vindication was not the same thing as restoration.

Judge Hayes looked toward the jury. “Ladies and gentlemen, the court thanks you for your service. You have carried out a difficult responsibility with care and seriousness. You are now released from your obligation as jurors in this case. You may speak about your service if you choose, but you are not required to do so. The court asks only that you continue to treat your duty, and one another, with the same seriousness you have shown throughout these proceedings.”

Several jurors lowered their eyes. Some looked relieved. Others looked as though release from the court’s instruction did not free them from what they had heard. Paul Jensen sat very still, his notebook resting against his knee. Leonard Shaw stared forward with an unreadable expression. Anthony Russo rubbed his thumb against the edge of his wedding ring. Rebecca Collins wiped quickly beneath one eye and looked down before anyone could notice.

Judge Hayes turned toward counsel. “The verdict is received and entered. This matter is concluded.”

The deputy called the court to order as Judge Hayes left the bench. Reporters began moving almost immediately. The gallery stirred. Some people embraced quietly. Others began whispering into phones. The courtroom that had held its breath for weeks released itself back into noise.

David stood and shook Professor Price's hand. "You stood well," he said.

Professor Price's eyes were moist. "So did you."

David shook his head slightly. "The evidence stood."

Professor Price looked toward the jury box, where the jurors had begun to gather their belongings. Some avoided eye contact. Others looked toward him with expressions that carried more than legal duty. He wanted to thank them, but he knew better than to approach unless they chose to speak. Their service was complete, and whatever had happened in the room behind the jury box might remain theirs alone.

Rebecca Kane closed her briefcase slowly. She heard voices around her, reporters calling her name, assistants asking whether she wanted to make a statement, but all of it seemed far away. She had lost cases before. Every trial lawyer had. This felt different. She did not feel defeated in the usual way. She felt exposed.

David approached her after speaking briefly with Professor Price. He did not come with a smile of victory or the posture of a man eager to remind her of the outcome. He waited until she looked up, then gave a small nod.

"Ms. Kane."

"Mr. Stone."

"You tried a strong case," David said.

Rebecca gave a faint, tired smile. "That is a generous thing to say after winning."

"It is a true thing to say."

She closed the latch on her briefcase. "The jury disagreed."

"The jury answered the legal question," David said. "That does not mean the questions you raised were unimportant."

Rebecca studied him for a moment. She had expected relief from him, perhaps satisfaction, perhaps guarded triumph. Instead, he seemed almost burdened by the verdict, as though he understood that winning a case about truth did not make truth easier for anyone.

"You really believe that, don't you?" she asked.

"Believe what?"

"That truth can survive being questioned."

David looked toward Professor Price, who was speaking quietly with Harold Bennett near the rail. "Yes. I do."

Rebecca looked down at the table. The old photograph of her father was inside her briefcase, tucked into an inner pocket where she had placed it after it slipped out days earlier. She could feel its presence without touching it. The trial had carried her closer to that picture than she wanted to admit.

"I used to believe that," she said.

David did not press her. He had cross-examined enough witnesses to know when silence was more useful than another question. Rebecca looked back at him after a moment, her voice quieter than before.

"I thought this case was about keeping religion from being dressed up as fact," she said. "I still think lines matter. I still think universities have responsibilities. But somewhere in the middle of all this, I realized I was not only arguing against

Professor Price. I was arguing against a version of God I learned to hate."

David's expression softened. "That is a harder case to try."

Rebecca let out a quiet breath that almost became a laugh. "Harder to win too."

David did not answer quickly. When he did, his voice remained low enough that the surrounding noise covered it. "Maybe some cases are not meant to be won the way we think."

Rebecca looked toward the jury box. Leonard was speaking with Anthony near the aisle. Paul stood alone for a moment, then turned and said something to Sheila. Rebecca could not hear the words, but she saw Sheila's face soften as she answered him. Something had happened among them. The verdict form had only recorded the legal conclusion, but their faces told her the deliberations had gone somewhere deeper.

Professor Price approached the defense table before Rebecca could leave. David stepped aside, allowing the moment to belong to them.

"Ms. Kane," Professor Price said.

Rebecca straightened slightly. "Professor Price."

He held her gaze with a kindness that almost unsettled her. "You argued with conviction."

"So did you."

"I know this was not easy."

She studied him, wondering whether he meant the trial or something else. "No," she said. "It was not."

Professor Price hesitated. "I want you to know I bear you no resentment."

Rebecca looked away briefly. She had been prepared for many responses from him, but not that one. "You would have had reason."

"Perhaps," he said. "But resentment would not serve the truth."

The words were not dramatic. They were not delivered for anyone else to hear. That was why they reached her. He did not sound like a man trying to appear gracious. He sounded like a man who had already decided before the verdict that bitterness would not own him.

Rebecca swallowed. "I don't know what to do with that."

Professor Price nodded. "Most of us don't, at first."

Outside the courthouse, cameras waited for statements, but Rebecca exited through a side corridor where the light was dimmer and the noise less severe. She stepped into the evening air alone, carrying her briefcase in one hand and her phone in the other. Behind her, the courthouse doors closed on the case of Price v. Northbridge University. Ahead of her, the city moved as it always had, full of traffic, voices, strangers, wounds, prayers, and unanswered questions.

The trial had decided one case. It had not answered every question. It had not healed every wound. It had not made truth simple. It had opened something Rebecca thought had been closed forever, and as she walked down the courthouse steps, she looked once more at her father's name on her phone.

# Epilogue

THREE MONTHS AFTER THE verdict, Professor Daniel Price returned to Northbridge University for the first time since the trial ended. The campus looked almost exactly as it had before the controversy began. Students crossed the courtyard with backpacks over their shoulders, professors moved quickly between buildings with coffee cups in hand, bicycles leaned against railings, and flyers for lectures, concerts, and student organizations covered the announcement boards near the humanities building. Life at the university had continued while the nation argued about his case, and for a moment that ordinary movement comforted him more than applause ever could. It reminded him that institutions could wound, but classrooms could still begin again.

He paused outside the lecture hall where everything had started. The door was open, and the room was already full. Some students had come because they supported him. Others had come because they disagreed with him. A few had come because the trial had made his name impossible to ignore. Professor Price understood all of it. He had never expected agreement from every student, and after the trial, he wanted agreement less than he wanted honesty.

David Stone stood in the back of the room. Professor Price had not asked him to come, but the sight of him steadied something inside him. David had fought the legal battle with skill, but more than that, he had carried the case without turning it into a war of arrogance. That mattered to Price. Winning the verdict had been important, but winning without humility would have betrayed the truth they had defended. David gave him a small nod, and Price returned it before stepping toward the podium.

When Professor Price reached the front of the room, the conversations faded. He placed his notes in front of him but did not open them immediately. He looked at the students, at the faces curious and skeptical, supportive and uncertain, and he thought of the twelve jurors who had sat through weeks of testimony and then gone behind a closed door to decide whether faith could be examined as truth. He also thought of the cost. A verdict could clear a man legally, but it could not make the past untouched.

"For several months," he said, "people have asked whether the trial changed what I believe. It did not change the substance of my convictions, but it reminded me that convictions must be held with humility. If truth is real, then honest questions do not threaten it. They test us, correct us, refine us, and sometimes expose the places where we have confused confidence with pride."

A student near the front raised his hand and asked whether Professor Price believed faith could really be based on evidence. It was the kind of question that might have sounded hostile before the trial, but now Price heard it differently. It was not enough for students to memorize conclusions. They needed permission to wrestle. They needed a classroom where disagreement was not treated as betrayal.

"I believe faith without evidence can become fragile," Price answered. "I also believe evidence without humility can become cold. The better path is to follow truth with both the mind and the conscience engaged. That does not mean every person will agree with me. It means the search itself deserves honesty."

David watched from the back as students began taking notes. He had seen verdicts change careers, reputations, and futures, but this case had done something different. It had reminded him that truth did not only win arguments. It entered rooms, opened wounds, challenged assumptions, and waited patiently for people to respond. He had spent his career studying how evidence moved juries, but this case had reminded him that evidence could move souls too.

Across town, Paul Jensen sat in the back row of a small church he had passed many times but had never entered before the trial. He had arrived late on purpose and chosen a seat close to the exit. The service had already begun when he slipped inside, and nobody turned around to stare. No one asked for his story. No one demanded that he know the right words. That helped more than he expected.

The pastor was teaching from the Gospel of John. Paul almost smiled when he realized it. He had started reading John two weeks after the verdict, partly because Professor Price had mentioned it during a televised interview and partly because Paul needed to know whether the Jesus he had spent years rejecting was anything like the Jesus presented in the text. He still had questions. He had questions about suffering, Scripture, hypocrisy, miracles, prayer, and the uncomfortable word surrender. But he had stopped using questions as a locked door.

When the pastor read, "I am the resurrection and the life," Paul lowered his eyes. A year earlier, the sentence would have sounded religious, excessive, and impossible. Now it sounded like the same question that had followed him from the jury room to his apartment and from his apartment into the quiet places of his mind. If He rose, what does that require of me? Paul did not yet have a polished answer, but he had begun to understand that not every true answer arrives polished.

After the service, an older man turned around and introduced himself. He did not ask Paul whether he was new in a way that made Paul feel exposed. He simply told him he was glad he had come and offered his hand. Paul shook it, waiting for the pressure, the sales pitch, or the demand for a testimony. None came. The man smiled, told him there was coffee in the lobby, and then walked away to speak with someone else. The kindness nearly undid Paul because it asked nothing from him except to receive it.

At Russo's, Anthony stood beside his brother Michael in the kitchen while the dinner rush gathered beyond the swinging doors. Pans clattered, garlic hit hot oil, and the line cooks moved with the practiced urgency of people who had done this too many times to panic. The restaurant had always been Anthony's refuge. Food made sense. If something burned, you started over. If a sauce needed salt, you added it. If a customer complained, you fixed what you could and moved on. Wounds of the soul were not that simple, and that had always made him angry.

Michael rolled dough beside him, slower than Anthony would have liked but steady enough. They had spoken more in the last three months than in the previous three years. Not every conversation had gone well. Some had ended in silence. One had ended with Anthony walking out into the alley behind the restaurant and punching a stack of empty boxes until his knuckles bled. But Michael kept coming back, and Anthony had started to understand that his brother's faith was not denial. It was survival of a different kind.

"You went again Sunday?" Anthony asked without looking at him.

Michael dusted flour across the counter. "I did."

Anthony pressed his palms into the dough harder than necessary. "I still don't understand how you can sit in church after what happened."

Michael did not answer quickly, and Anthony appreciated that. Quick answers had always sounded rehearsed to him. "I don't go because I forgot what happened," Michael said. "I go because I don't want the man who hurt me to own every place where God's name is spoken. For years, he owned too much. I am trying to take some of it back."

Anthony stopped working the dough. The kitchen noise continued around them, but for a moment it seemed distant. "I don't know if I can do that."

Michael looked at him with gentleness that carried no weakness. "You don't have to do it today."

Anthony nodded and returned to the dough, but something in him had shifted. He was not ready to forgive the man who hurt his brother. He was not ready to walk into church. He was not ready to pray in words that felt sincere. But for the first time, he wondered if his anger at God had also kept him chained to the man he hated. That possibility disturbed him, but it also gave him the faintest sense that another door might exist.

In a quiet neighborhood across the city, Leonard Shaw stood at his mother's grave with his hands buried in the pockets of his coat. He had not visited in almost a year. Work had been the excuse. Weather had been the excuse. The truth was simpler and harder to admit. Her grave reminded him of everything unresolved: the bathroom water running, the makeup beneath her eye, the Bible beside her bed, and the way she kept going to church when Leonard thought any reasonable person would have burned the place down.

He had brought her Bible with him, the one he had found in the box after the day of deliberations. It was still cracked at the spine, and several pages had loosened near the Psalms. He had not read it during the trial, but after the verdict, he had opened it one evening and discovered notes in the margins. His mother's handwriting was smaller than he remembered. Beside one verse, she had written, Lord, help me endure without becoming bitter. Beside another, she had written, Protect my children. That note had broken him in a way anger never had.

Leonard stood by the grave for a long time before speaking. He did not know whether he was talking to his mother, to God, or to the boy he had once been. "I thought you were weak," he said. "I thought praying meant you were pretending everything was fine. I didn't know you were fighting to stay alive inside."

The wind moved lightly through the trees, and Leonard hated himself for expecting something more. A sign. A voice. A feeling strong enough to settle what the trial had disturbed. None came. The cemetery remained a cemetery. The grass moved. Cars passed on the road beyond the fence. The world did not stop because Leonard Shaw had finally spoken honestly at his mother's grave.

He looked down at the Bible in his hands. "I still don't know what I believe," he said. "But if You were with her in that house, then maybe I was wrong about more than I want to admit."

He stood there until the light began to fade, then placed his palm against the top of the stone before leaving. He did not feel converted. He did not feel healed. He no longer felt certain that anger had told him the whole truth.

Evelyn Brooks had started attending a small Wednesday afternoon prayer gathering at a church not far from her home. She did not tell many people. She still sat near the back, and she still left quickly when people became too eager to welcome her. Yet she returned each week. At first, she told herself she was going because she missed music or because the people were kind. Eventually she admitted the deeper reason. She missed hope, and hope had started to feel possible again.

One afternoon, after everyone left, Evelyn remained in the sanctuary and walked to the front pew. Her husband's death had taught her how loud absence could be. For thirty years, she had mistaken the ache for proof that God had left. Now she was beginning to wonder if grief had not been evidence of absence, but evidence that love was too large to be erased by death. She sat down and let the quiet gather around her without trying to fill it.

She bowed her head and prayed for the first time without feeling as though she had betrayed her sorrow. "I am still sad," she whispered. "But I am here."

The prayer was simple, and that simplicity felt honest enough.

Rebecca Collins kept the drawing of the open door pinned above her desk. At first, she had thought it was only a sketch made during an emotional season. But weeks passed, and she did not take it down. The door remained slightly open, the line of light spilling across the floor. She had tried to redraw it several times, but none of the later versions felt as true as the first. That one had been made before she knew what she was drawing.

She began attending a discussion group at a church near her apartment, not because she was ready to call herself Christian, but because the questions had become too alive to ignore. The group was reading the Gospel of Luke. Rebecca liked Luke because he sounded careful. He wrote like someone who had investigated things. That mattered to her. She still felt awkward when people prayed. She did not know when to close her eyes, what to do with her hands, or whether silence meant something was supposed to happen. But she kept coming.

One night after the group, a woman asked what brought her there. Rebecca looked at the open Bible in front of her and thought of the jury room, of Paul saying he had dismissed what he had not examined, and of Harold saying a door could open before you knew it had been closed.

"I think I saw a door," Rebecca said. "I'm trying to find out where it leads."

The woman did not laugh. She simply nodded, as though that answer made perfect sense.

Maria Alvarez returned to her classroom with a different kind of caution. She still taught history carefully. She still taught her students to examine sources, recognize bias, weigh evidence, and resist easy answers. But when she reached the unit on the first century, she no longer rushed past Jesus as though neutrality required distance from significance. She taught Him as a real figure in a real place, surrounded by real tensions, followed by real people who believed real events had changed history.

A student asked whether Maria believed the resurrection happened. Before the trial, she would have deflected. She would have said the classroom was not the place for personal belief. She still believed that students should not be pressured by a teacher's convictions, but the trial had taught her that hiding every conviction was not the same as fairness. She answered carefully, not to persuade the student but to honor the question.

"I believe the question deserves serious examination," she said. "And I believe no honest student should be afraid to follow the evidence wherever it leads."

Later that afternoon, alone in her classroom, Maria looked at the map of the ancient Mediterranean and let her eyes rest on Judea. For years, she had taught the region as geography. Now it felt like an address.

Patricia Nguyen continued to attend family gatherings, light incense with her mother on certain days, and honor the traditions that had shaped her. She did not discard them lightly, and she did not treat her questions as rebellion. But she had begun reading the New Testament in private, not out of shame, but out of reverence for the weight of what she was doing. She started with Matthew, then moved to John because Paul had told her he was reading it.

Her mother noticed the book one evening on the kitchen table. "You are studying Jesus."

Patricia looked up, startled. "Yes."

Her mother sat across from her. "Are you afraid I will be disappointed?"

Patricia hesitated. The answer was yes, but the word felt too small. "I don't want to dishonor you."

Her mother reached across the table and touched her hand. "If truth is calling you, listen carefully. Honor is not pretending you do not hear."

Patricia's eyes filled, and she looked back down at the page. She had not become a Christian yet. She had not crossed that line. But the line was no longer somewhere far away. It was in front of her, and she was learning that truth sometimes approached slowly so a person could count the cost.

Denise Walker kept working, kept praying, and kept carrying grief with both hands. The trial had not made her faith easier. It had made it more honest. When families asked why, she no longer felt the need to fill every silence. Sometimes she simply sat with them. Sometimes she prayed. Sometimes she said she did not know. Beneath the not knowing, there was a steadiness that had grown stronger since the verdict.

One night, after a child in her former unit took a sudden turn for the worse, Denise drove to the hospital and sat with the mother while doctors worked. The mother kept asking whether God heard her. Denise held her hand and did not offer an explanation she could not defend. "I believe He hears," Denise said. "And I believe He is near, even when I do not understand."

The mother leaned into her and wept. Denise wept too. She had learned that faith did not require dry eyes.

Marcus Reed reopened a cold case that had haunted him for seven years. He did not reopen it because of a dream or a sign. He reopened it because the trial had reminded him that truth mattered even when justice was delayed. If there was a Judge beyond this life, Marcus still believed the judges in this life had work to do. Hope was not permission to neglect evidence. It was strength to keep pursuing it.

Late one evening, he sat at his desk reading through old interviews when he found a discrepancy he had missed before. It was small, but not meaningless. A time. A location. A statement that did not match the original report. Marcus circled it and leaned back in his chair, feeling again the stubborn pull of truth.

He thought of Professor Price, of the jury room, and of the phrase he had not said aloud to anyone. Final justice may belong to God, but present justice still matters. Then he picked up the phone and called the prosecutor assigned to the case.

Frank Dawson and his wife Ellen began taking evening walks again. They had done that years earlier, before work, age, and routine slowly reduced the practice to something they remembered fondly but rarely did. After the trial, Frank found himself wanting quiet that moved. Walking helped. So did

Ellen's presence. She never asked him to explain more than he could, but she listened when he tried.

One evening, they passed a church with its doors open for a midweek service. Music drifted faintly onto the sidewalk. Frank slowed but did not stop.

Ellen looked at him. "Do you want to go in?"

Frank smiled. "Not tonight."

She nodded, and they kept walking.

After a few steps, Frank added, "Maybe Sunday."

Ellen did not make too much of it. She simply took his hand, and that was enough.

Harold Bennett wrote letters to three of the jurors. He wrote one to Paul, one to Anthony, and one to Leonard. He did not mail any of them immediately. He had learned long ago that not every true word needed to be delivered at once. Sometimes prayer was the better envelope. He kept the letters in his desk drawer and prayed over them each morning, asking God to show him whether to send them or simply keep loving the men from a distance.

The letter to Leonard was the shortest. It said only that Harold was honored to have served with him, that questions did not disqualify a man from grace, and that the God Leonard wished was better than his father truly was. Harold read the letter several times and left it unsent. He suspected Leonard was not ready for it, and love required enough patience to wait.

Sheila Morrison began meeting Rebecca Collins for coffee every other Thursday. Rebecca had asked the first time with visible embarrassment, saying she did not need counseling, only someone safe to ask questions. Sheila agreed immediately. They talked about prayer, Scripture, doubt, church wounds, and what it meant to seek truth without pretending certainty had arrived all at once.

During one of those meetings, Rebecca asked whether Sheila had always believed.

Sheila smiled at the question. "I have believed for a long time. But belief has not always felt the same. Sometimes it felt like joy. Sometimes it felt like obedience. Sometimes it felt like holding on with tired hands."

Rebecca stirred her coffee. "That sounds more honest than what I expected faith to be."

"It is honest," Sheila said. "Faith is not pretending the storm is not real. It is trusting the One who is with you in it."

Rebecca looked out the window and thought again of the open door above her desk.

Rebecca Kane did not call her father the day after the verdict. She did not call him the next week either. The voicemail remained saved on her phone, and several times she played it in her car without responding. His voice sounded older each time. Proud of you. I pray for you every day. I love you, sweetheart. The words did not erase the past. They did not undo the affair, the divorce, the church split, or the years of silence. But they no longer sounded like manipulation. They sounded like regret.

Nearly four months after the verdict, she drove to the small church where her father still preached. She did not go inside. She parked across the street and watched people enter for the evening service. He stood near the door, greeting them slowly, one hand resting on a cane she did not know he used. He looked smaller than she remembered. That startled her. In her anger, he had remained large, almost mythic, the man who ruined everything. Seeing him older did not excuse him, but it made him human again.

She sat in the car until the service began. Then she picked up her phone and called him. Through the church windows, she saw him reach into his coat pocket. He looked at the screen and froze. For a moment, Rebecca thought he would not answer. Then he stepped away from the door and lifted the phone to his ear.

"Rebecca?"

His voice broke on her name.

She closed her eyes. "Hi, Dad."

Neither spoke for several seconds. Rebecca had imagined this call many times, and in every version she was stronger, angrier, more prepared. Now she had nothing polished to say.

"I don't know what this is," she said. "I'm not ready to talk about everything. I'm not ready to pretend I'm not angry. But I listened to your message."

On the other side of the street, her father lowered his head. "Thank you for calling."

The humility in his voice hurt more than defensiveness would have. Rebecca looked down at the photograph on the passenger seat, the one from years ago in front of the church, the one she had carried through the trial like evidence of betrayal. It was still evidence of pain, but it was no longer only that.

"I have questions," she said.

"I know."

"I don't just mean about you."

Her father looked through the church window toward the sanctuary, then back toward the dark street, not knowing she was parked across from him. "I know that too."

Rebecca wiped at her eyes with the back of her hand. "I don't know if I can come in."

"You don't have to."

"I don't know if I can forgive you."

"I know."

"I don't know if I believe like I used to."

Her father's voice softened. "Then start with the truth you have."

Rebecca looked across the street at the church doors. For years, she had thought returning would mean surrendering the validity of her pain. Now she wondered if healing might begin by telling the truth about it in the presence of a God who had never asked her to lie.

"I can sit in the parking lot," she said.

"Then I'll stay on the phone with you from the doorway."

For the first time in years, Rebecca laughed through tears. It was small and broken, but it was real.

At Northbridge University, Professor Price finished his lecture and gathered his notes while students formed a line to speak with him. Some thanked him. Some challenged him. One told him he still disagreed with almost everything but appreciated being taken seriously. Price thanked each of them. He did not need them to leave convinced. He wanted them to leave awakened to the weight of the questions.

When the room finally emptied, David Stone approached from the back.

"How did it feel?" David asked.

Professor Price looked around the lecture hall. "Like beginning again."

David smiled. "That is not a bad thing."

"No," Price said. "It is not."

They walked out together into the late afternoon. The campus was alive with movement, argument, laughter, and the ordinary restlessness of young minds. Professor Price paused near the courtyard and watched a group of students debate something with great intensity near the steps. He could not hear the subject, but he liked the sight of it.

Truth had not become easier after the trial. It rarely does. But it had been given room to breathe. Somewhere across the city, in churches, apartments, restaurants, classrooms, cemeteries, hospitals, kitchens, and parked cars, the verdict continued in quieter ways. Not everyone had arrived at faith. Not every wound had healed. Not every question had been answered. But doors had opened. Some only a crack, some wider than expected.

For those willing to keep seeking, the trial had done more than decide whether one professor could speak. It had reminded them that truth does not fear examination, that grace does not deny pain, and that the question of Jesus Christ cannot be buried forever beneath anger, assumption, or doubt. Some verdicts are read in courtrooms. Others unfold slowly in the human heart.

www.ingramcontent.com/pod-product-compliance
Lightning Source LLC
LaVergne TN
LVHW100256210926
848480LV00003B/934

* 9 7 9 8 9 9 6 2 2 7 2 4 2 *